## FURTHER PRAISE FOR *THE JOB-EMBEDDED NATURE OF COACHING*

"In her persistent and thoughtful way, Dr. Sally J. Zepeda has seamlessly brought research and practice together to describe, analyze, and develop ideas around coaching for successful teaching and leading. Her work is characteristically informed from research experts who happen also to be doing the real work of schooling every day. It is the capacity for having one foot in the research litera- ture and one foot in the practice of teaching and leading, that we find a refreshing and somewhat unique approach to developing teachers and leaders. Dr. Zepeda has managed never to lose her bearing when it comes to writing in authentic and impactful ways. Her cadre of writers, experts from the field who have done their own independent research, reflect that grounded approach and as a consequence, the reader enjoys a thoughtful, relevant, and meaningful narrative.

There is also a special quality to this writing that reflects Dr. Zepeda's world view, I suspect. When we read her work, and the work of her collaborators, we come away with this idea, an audacious assumption, that we all have the capacity for remarkable work and if we are reflective, careful, and engaged, then our chil- dren will act similarly. Imagine that: a school culture where leaders, teachers, and students are reflective, caring, and engaged. Dr. Zepeda offers us a way to be such a place." —**Zach Kelehear**, dean of the College of Education and vice president for instruction and innovation, Augusta University

"Another grand-slam, home-run for Dr. Sally Zepeda! This amazing book is a much needed 'wake up' call and guide to coaching, especially considering the high attrition rate for new teachers. Administrators, teacher leaders, professional development directors, and anyone working with new teachers and coaching have long anticipated the clear, concise presentation of practical ideas and strat- egies. Numerous strategies, focused on the conservation and belongingness needed to retain and develop novice teachers, are illuminated in this body of work. The insights and direction provided by the authors are timely and highly applicable to any setting. This book is a valuable reference and a must-read for anyone involved in coaching." —**Dr. Lauren D. Rentfro**, associate professor and program director, secondary, middle level, and foreign language education, Lewis University College of Education

# The Job-Embedded Nature of Coaching

## BRIDGING THEORY AND PRACTICE

This international series reflects the latest cutting-edge theories and practices in school leadership. Uniquely, we include books that bridge the perennial divide between theory and practice. The series motto is framed after Kurt Lewin's famous statement, and we paraphrase, that there is no sound theory without practice, and no good practice that is not framed on some theory.

# The Job-Embedded Nature of Coaching

## Lessons and Insights for School Leaders at All Levels

Sally J. Zepeda

ROWMAN & LITTLEFIELD
Lanham • Boulder • New York • London

Published by Rowman & Littlefield
A wholly owned subsidiary of The Rowman & Littlefield Publishing Group, Inc.
4501 Forbes Boulevard, Suite 200, Lanham, Maryland 20706
www.rowman.com

Unit A, Whitacre Mews, 26-34 Stannary Street, London SE11 4AB

British Library Cataloguing in Publication Information Available

**Library of Congress Cataloging-in-Publication Data Available**
Library of Congress Control Number: 2018953772
ISBN 978-1-4758-4326-2 (cloth : alk. paper)
ISBN 978-1-4758-4327-9 (pbk. : alk. paper)
ISBN 978-1-4758-4328-6 (electronic)

Printed in the United States of America

# Contents

# About the Rowman & Littlefield Series on School Leadership

Why another book series on school leadership, and what does this particular series have to offer among the many fine books already published in the field of school leadership?

Research over the past decade has confirmed what many educators, policy makers, think tanks, and others viscerally knew—that leadership makes a difference for a host of dependent variables, including the most important one, student achievement. Additional research is needed, however, to more fully refine and uncover how, in fact, school leaders make a difference.

The Rowman & Littlefield School Leadership Series is premised on the need to connect theory to practice. This international series, in other words, reflects the latest cutting-edge theories and practices in school leadership that attempt to bridge the perennial divide between theory and practice.

The Series motto is framed after Kurt Lewin's famous statement, and we paraphrase, that there is no sound theory without practice, and no good practice that is not framed on some theory. We look for manuscripts that are intellectually engaging, with a sound theoretical base, yet firmly grounded in the daily lives of school leaders. I welcome readers to join the effort to increase knowledge in our field and affect daily school practice by submitting a proposal on any of the topics mentioned, or any other relevant ones. Feel free to communicate with the series editor via email at yosglanz@gmail.com

As Series Editor, I take this opportunity to thank the Advisory Board for their efforts. Their feedback to the editor were instrumental in crafting a well-researched, practical, and readable volume.

**Yin Cheong Cheng**, The Education University of Hong Kong, Tai Po, Hong Kong
**Mary Lynne Derrington**, University of Tennessee, Knoxville, TN, USA

**Francis M. Duffy**, Gallaudet University, Washington DC, USA
**Sedat Gumus**, Necmettin Erbakan University, Konya, Turkey
**Helen M. Hazi**, West Virginia University at Morgantown, West Virginia, USA
**Albert Jimenez,** Kennesaw State University, Kennesaw, GA, USA
**Philip D. Lanoue,** PDL Consultants, Marietta, SC, USA (Former principal/superintendent)
**Chen Schechter**, Bar Ilan University, Ramat Gan, Israel
**Duncan Waite**, Texas State University, San Marcos, Texas, USA
**Jane Wilkinson**, Monash University, Victoria, Australia
**Sally J. Zepeda**, University of Georgia, Athens, GA, USA

Special acknowledgement is extended to Tom Koerner (Vice President and Publisher for Education Issues), Carlie Wall (Managing Editor), and Emily Tuttle (Assistant Editor) for their support. Special thanks to Sue Canavan of the former Christopher-Gordon Publishers for first shepherding the idea for this series. I hope this volume and the series will receive wide acknowledgement for making a difference in the field of educational leadership.

# Volume Introduction

As Series Editor, I am excited to present *The Job-Embedded Nature of Coaching: Lessons and Insights for School Leaders at All Levels*, a book for sitting principals, aspiring principals, and teacher–leaders. This edited volume includes three studies that describe and detail findings from dissertation research conducted by scholar–practitioners in pre-K–12 schools. This book makes unique contributions to the field of practice and understanding of coaching (instructional and peer coaching) as forms of job-embedded learning, most especially for teachers in the beginning years in the profession. Each chapter examines specific aspects of coaching that school leaders need to have an understanding about to be able to create systems that support teachers in the work they do to teach students, interact with colleagues, etc. Conclusions and recommendations are offered for school leaders to support an environment and culture that embraces coaching and job-embedded learning as an integral part of the school's foundation for building capacity. The messages across the chapters point to the primacy of coaching to promote teacher engagement and its value as job-embedded learning.

Sally J. Zepeda's edited volume fits in beautifully with the intended purpose of the R&L School Leadership Series and is an excellent example of our goal to connect theory with practice.

Although this book is not primarily focused in the international context, I think its ideas are indeed relevant to schools all over the world. Job-embedded learning, especially in terms of coaching, has been highlighted in the literature of educational leadership. *The Job-Embedded Nature of Coaching: Lessons and Insights for School Leaders at All Levels* takes us to a new level of understanding that surpasses the confines of schooling in a limited context. Lessons gleaned from this work are timely, practical, and theoretically grounded.

Professor Zepeda is among the top scholars in the field, if not the very top. Her productivity is astounding. She has made a significant impression in our field, and I am personally honored that she consented to contribute to our series with this new book.

Jeffrey Glanz, Series Editor
March 5, 2018

# Preface

*The Job-Embedded Nature of Coaching: Lessons and Insights for School Leaders at All Levels* is a book for sitting principals and assistant principals aspiring to the principalship. However, teacher–leaders, regardless of role (e.g., lead teacher, mentor, department chair), can gain insights from the case studies about coaching that are presented in this book. These insights can support school and system efforts to build coaching programs, to prepare and support coaches, but more importantly, to gain the benefits that coaching can provide to teachers who have a profound and direct influence on student learning.

This book is timely because schools face many challenges centering on professional learning—austerity cuts from state and federal sources and programs, the inclusion of professional learning as part of teacher evaluation systems, and even more unfortunate, the inferior quality of most professional learning where teachers play the role of spectator, benched until they can return to their classrooms too often without the motivation to implement what they endured. The research is clear that coaching with fidelity can make a difference, ensuring transfer of what is learned into practice, reducing isolation, and increasing collaboration.

The cases in this edited book are important for three interrelated reasons. First, the chapters examine specific aspects of coaching that school leaders need to have an understanding of to be able to create systems that support teachers, most especially ones new to the profession. As the profession of teaching becomes more complex and unattractive given its demands and the almost unreasonable and unrealistic roles being cast for them to fulfill, school leaders must be in the position to work with teachers, keeping them engaged and motivated about their own learning. Teacher shortages show no sign of slowing down and the numbers have been consistent; we lose too many teachers at the onset of their careers.

Second, the steady proliferation of coaching in pre-K–12 schools also makes this book a timely one. School leaders must be able to bring coherence to professional learning by adding supports offered to teachers during the workday. It is imperative for school leaders to understand how job-embedded learning vis-à-vis coaching can support teacher growth and development, how school-wide programs can nurture teachers from the very newest to the veteran, and how peer coaches can support the work of leaders in fostering a culture of learning within their buildings. These and other ideas will be amplified throughout the chapters in this book.

Third, coaching is an important part in the equation for embedding professional learning as a daily part of a teacher's professional duty. Teaching and learning to teach is complex and occurs across the career continuum. We need teachers who can learn not only from their own work but also with others in team settings, in the classrooms of their colleagues, and through other arrangements. To engage teachers in learning, professional development must move beyond the predictable pattern of the "sit, get, and hope something sticks" mentality.

Coaching offers our best hope for bringing coherence to embed learning as a daily practice for teachers. The job-embedded nature of coaching can go a long way in combatting isolation, supporting the exchange of feedback and conversations about practices that unfold in classrooms, and engaging coaches and teachers in forms of learning to teach through, for example, co-teaching, co-planning, modeling, reflecting, engaging in action research, etc.

Each chapter is based on dissertation research conducted in schools that are representative of the variance found in pre-K–12 schools regardless of location—urban, suburban, and rural contexts—or state. The chapter authors bring credibility through their experiences as classroom teachers, instructional coaches, and school administrators across elementary, middle, and high school. From their chapters, the reader will draw insights from the rich portrayals of coaching as a conduit for job-embedded learning.

## KEY FEATURES IN THE CHAPTERS

To support readability, each chapter includes key sections:

- a scenario,
- a highlight of the key ideas within the chapter,
- an abstract,
- an overview of the key literature related to the study,

- the context of the study,
- a brief review of the research methods,
- the presentation of findings,
- a discussion of findings, and then,
- implications for school leaders.

The chapters then end with discussion questions and suggested readings to support ongoing reflection and conversations about professional learning. The references follow.

# Acknowledgments

Many people worked behind the scenes to support this effort. From the University of Georgia, research assistant Sevda Yidirim, who is working on the Doctor of Philosophy Degree in the Department of Lifelong Education, Administration, and Policy. Sevda supported all efforts, and I am indebted to her work ethic, commitment, and good will.

A special thank you is extended to Dr. Tom Koerner, Vice President and Publisher for Education Issues at Rowman & Littlefield; Carlie Wall, Managing Editor; and Emily Tuttle, Assistant Editor. What a great team!

I am humbled by Dr. Jeffrey Glanz, series editor, for his leadership and encouragement to move forward with this project. Jeffrey gave solid feedback to the proposal and the final manuscript. I have known Jeffrey for more than twenty-five years, and he has always been a champion for high-quality work.

To the chapter authors, without your dedication to the profession, this edited book would not have been possible. It is with immense pride that I present your individual works and this collective that holds promise to support the efforts of teachers, leaders, and the schools in which job-embedded coaching can make a difference.

*1*

# Coaching in the Context of Job-Embedded Professional Learning

## Sally J. Zepeda

Key Ideas in This Chapter

- Job-Embedded Professional Learning
- Coaching
- Instructional Coaching
- Peer Coaching
- Coaching New Teachers
- Overview of Chapters

## INTRODUCTION

Schools are "complex systems with many moving parts" according to Danielson (2009, p. 3) and from the research, quality teaching goes a long way to improve student learning outcomes. Effective teachers continue to be the single-most crucial factor in raising student achievement (Hanushek & Rivkin, 2010). Given the impact teachers can have on student growth and development, it makes sense to focus time and effort to ensure that teachers are engaged daily in learning from their work with students and alongside their colleagues.

This edited book includes three studies that describe and detail findings from dissertation research conducted by scholar-practitioners in pre-K–12 schools and their systems. The focus of this book is broadly on coaching—peer coaching and instructional coaching. These three studies offer an in-depth view of coaching as a form of job-embedded learning. We get to see and learn about:

- How peer coaching evolved to support first-year teachers who were part of a learning community;
- The perspectives that first-year teachers offered about the conversations they had with their instructional coaches; and
- The perspectives that instructional coaches had about their work coaching teachers.

Conclusions and recommendations are offered for school leaders to support an environment that embraces coaching as a form of job-embedded learning. The messages from within and across the chapters point to the value and utility of coaching to engage teachers in job-embedded learning from the very work they do in their classrooms and the interactions they have with their peers.

To position the messages offered by the chapter authors, this one examines the key principles and constructs associated with job-embedded professional learning and coaching. Although the context in which coaching evolves is critical, the needs of new teachers are examined as is the essential support that leaders must provide to combat teacher attrition and isolation. The chapter ends with a broad overview of three cases that detail coaching.

## JOB-EMBEDDED PROFESSIONAL LEARNING

Job-embedded professional development occurs through the work of learning to teach in collaboration with teachers primarily at the site. When teachers engage in job-embedded learning, their learning is closely connected and aligned with the actual work of classroom practice through collaboration, and support of colleagues and others such as instructional coaches and school leaders. Job-embedded learning is relevant, promotes collegiality, enhances reflection, combats isolation, and provides timely feedback that facilitates the transfer of new skills into practice which should be the objective of all professional development (Zepeda 2012). These same characteristics are applicable to coaching.

Croft and colleagues (2010) define job-embedded professional development as "teacher learning that is grounded in day-to-day teaching practice and is designed to enhance teachers' content-specific instructional practices with the intent of improving student learning" (p. 2). The foundations of job-embedded learning set the stage for teachers to engage in learning that is

- Collaborative and reflective: teachers work with each other to address questions or problems of practice situated in the context of the classroom, within a grade level or across grade levels; they engage in discussions

about their practices and support reflection and inquiry about the impact of practices on student growth (Cochran-Smith & Lytle, 2009; Dana & Yendol-Hoppey, 2009; Feiman-Nemser, 2012a);
- Situated in classroom practices: teachers address the complexities of teaching and learning with students (Zepeda, 2015);
- Replete with support structures built into the process: teachers, coaches, and school leaders work in tandem to provide support through modeling, coaching, and mentoring to ensure learning from practice occurs (Desimone, 2011; Desimone & Garet, 2015; Zepeda, 2015, 2018);
- Engaging and personalized: teachers find value in the learning because they are engaged in learning that is personalized; teachers actively are engaged in designing, managing, and assessing their learning in the company of others (Darling-Hammond, Hyler, & Gardner, 2017; Desimone, 2011).

To be effective, job-embedded learning needs to focus on content (Darling-Hammond, Sutcher, & Carver-Thomas, 2017), build teacher knowledge about how students learn (Dana & Yendol-Hoppey, 2009), and include a focus on analyzing the artifacts of teaching and learning (Darling-Hammond, Wei, Andree, Richardson, & Orphanos, 2009; Desimone & Garet, 2015). The forms and processes of job-embedded learning situate teachers as the major actors in their own growth and development while supporting the same with their colleagues. There are many forms of job-embedded learning that include, for example, action research, peer coaching, book studies, etc.

On December 10, 2015, President Barack Obama signed the Every Student Succeeds Act (ESSA) into law, reauthorizing the Elementary and Secondary Education Act of 1965 and its most immediate predecessor, the No Child Left Behind Act of 2001. The language in ESSA surrounding professional learning is clear in its intents and definitions as found in Section 8101, 400-402, 42 A-(42) PROFESSIONAL DEVELOPMENT. —The term "professional development" means activities that—

(A) are an integral part of school and local educational agency strategies for providing educators (including teachers, principals, other school leaders, specialized instructional support personnel, paraprofessionals, and, as applicable, early childhood educators) with the knowledge and skills necessary to enable students to succeed in a well-rounded education and to meet the challenging State academic standards; and
(B) are sustained (not stand-alone, 1-day, or short-term workshops), intensive, collaborative, job-embedded, data-driven, and classroom-focused, and may include activities that—
  (i) improve and increase teachers'—

  (I) knowledge of the academic subjects the teachers teach;

  (II) understanding of how students learn; and,

  (III) ability to analyze student work and achievement from multiple sources, including how to adjust instructional strategies, assessments, and materials based on such analysis;

 (ii) are an integral part of broad school-wide and districtwide educational improvement plans;

 (iii) allow personalized plans for each educator to address the educator's specific needs identified in observation or other feedback;

 (iv) improve classroom management skills;

 (v) support the recruitment, hiring, and training of effective teachers, including teachers who became certified through State and local alternative routes to certification;

 (vi) advance teacher understanding of—

  (I) effective instructional strategies that are evidence-based; and

  (II) strategies for improving student academic achievement or substantially increasing the knowledge and teaching skills of teachers;

 (vii) are aligned with, and directly related to, academic goals of the school or local educational agency;

 (viii) are developed with extensive participation of teachers, principals, other school leaders, parents, representatives of Indian tribes (as applicable), and administrators of schools to be served under this Act (Every Student Succeeds Act of 2015).

The tenor of the legislation is clear about the primacy of high-quality professional learning that is job embedded.

## COACHING

What's in a name? It is common to hear educators speak of coaches—instructional coaches, literacy coaches, cognitive coaches, math coaches, peer coaches, and so on. For the purposes of this chapter and book, coaching is examined broadly and then focused on two models—instructional coaching and peer coaching.

Regardless of its form (e.g., peer coaching, instructional coaching, cognitive coaching), coaching supports job-embedded learning. Aguilar (2013) promoted that

> Coaching is an essential component of an effective professional development program. Coaching can build will, skill, knowledge, and capacity because it can

go where no other professional development has gone before: into the intellect, behaviors, practices, beliefs, values, and feelings of an educator. (p. 8)

## Background of Coaching

Coaching is complex because it is contextually situated in schools made up of teachers who work with a wide array of students, parents, leaders, and others within the building, system, and community. The complexity is the opportunity to develop a frame of reference to what coaching can become with the right supports. The stakes are high for teachers and the students they teach.

Coaching is an individualized, differentiated, and dynamic approach to professional learning that supports teachers regardless of career stage, length in the profession, or background preparation. At its best, coaching is contextualized and highly personalized because the interactive nature of coaching provides "opportunity to tailor information and guidance to a teacher's knowledge, skills, and specific classroom circumstances" (Powell & Diamond, 2013, p. 103).

Coaching has been described as:

- "hands-on, in-classroom assistance with the transfer of skills and strategies to the classroom" (Joyce & Showers, 1980, p. 380);
- a "stagecoach" taking teachers from where they are to the place where they desire to be (Costa & Garmston, 2015);
- a form of in-class support that uses reflection on practice to enhance competence (Veenman & Denessen, 2001);
- "the art of creating an environment, through conversation and a way of being, that facilitates the process by which a person can move toward desired goals in a fulfilling manner" (Gallwey, 2000, p. 177); and
- "doing, thinking, and being: doing a set of actions, holding a set of beliefs, and being in a way that results in those actions leading to change" (Aguilar, 2013, p. 20).

Coaching is an action-oriented change strategy that promotes growth and enhances professionalism.

Broadly, coaching involves:

- Supporting teachers in the development of deeper understanding of content knowledge;
- Extending thought processes needed to see different points of view about strategies;

- Helping develop critical-thinking skills through problem posing and problem-solving to get at looking at the impact of instruction on student success;
- Helping teachers boost student performance;
- Providing translations of research and making connections to classroom practice; and,
- Giving feedback on performance to answer the question, "Are we getting closer to meeting the objectives?" (Zepeda, 2012, pp. 65–66)

# INSTRUCTIONAL COACHING

Instructional coaching as a professional development model is a research-based approach that has gained momentum most notably through the efforts of James Knight (2005, 2008, 2011, 2015). An instructional coach, as defined by Knight (2005), is "an on-site professional developer who teaches educators how to use proven teaching methods" (p. 17). Coaches collaborate with teachers to identify practices that will effectively address teachers' needs and help them to implement these practices and newly learned skills (Joyce & Showers, 1996; Knight, 2005).

Instructional coaching also allows for improved instruction by providing a variety of learning experiences that builds individual capacity for change (Cobb & Jackson, 2011; Vanderburg & Stephens, 2010). Mangin and Dunsmore (2015) share that instructional coaches as staff developers engage in activities such as "modeling lessons, observing and providing feedback, or facilitating learning for groups of teachers such as grade- or subject-level teams (p. 5).

Effective instructional coaching programs are built on the relationships that coaches have with teachers. Knowing content, the curriculum, or a bevy of instructional strategies to share is simply not enough for instructional coaching (Knight, 2011). Instructional coaches give additional support for teachers. Knight (2015) reminds us that "[e]ffective coaches usually are good listeners, ask questions, build emotional connections, find common ground, build trust, and redirect destructive interactions" (p. 23).

The corpus of work by Knight (2007, 2008, 2011) shows instructional coaching is based on a partnership approach built on seven core principles highlighted in Table 1.1.

The principles of the partnership approach illustrate that coaching at its best is centered on collaboration and shared power.

**Table 1.1. Knight's Seven Principles of the Partnership Approach to Coaching**

| *Principles of the Partnership Approach* | *Brief Description* |
| --- | --- |
| Equality | Coaches communicate respect by acknowledging that teachers have an equal amount to contribute to collaboration. The relationship between the coach and the teacher is built on respect. |
| Choice | Teachers choose their coaching goals and decide which practices to adopt and how to interpret data. |
| Voice | Teachers are comfortable expressing their thoughts and concerns without fear of repercussions. |
| Reflection | Time for reflective conversations is provided. Teachers are encouraged to reflect on ideas and practices before adopting them as well as to participate in reflective discussions while implementing them. |
| Dialogue | Together the coach and the teacher arrive at the best idea through the interactive dialogue. |
| Praxis | Teachers are afforded time to apply new knowledge and skills in their classrooms with feedback. |
| Reciprocity | The coach and teacher are both open to learn together, and they are both engaged as both teachers and learners. The coach and the teacher are co-learners, each learning something about practice and its application. |

# PEER COACHING

In a peer-coaching model, teachers work together in partnership with each other to question and provide feedback related to elements of teaching (Joyce & Showers, 1996). Within this collaborative model, Joyce and Showers (1996) share that coaches engage in a variety of tasks, including planning instructional objectives, developing curricular and instructional materials, and collecting data about peer-coaching implementation processes and its effects. Peer coaching also includes engaging teachers in conversations before and after visiting classrooms.

Peer coaching emerged in the 1980s with the pioneering work of Joyce and Showers (1981, 1982). Coaching evolved to help teachers make new skills active parts of their instructional repertoire while helping them improve their instructional effectiveness through feedback and reflection. Joyce and Showers (1982) detailed the five major functions of the coaching process:

- provision of companionship: Coaching combats isolation.
- giving of technical feedback: Coaches, regardless of title, can observe teachers in their classrooms, give feedback, and actively promote reflection and inquiry about instructional practices.
- analysis of application: Through guided conversations, coaches can help teachers analyze their practices.
- adaptation to the students: Coaches support teachers in furthering their understandings of the students they teach.
- personal facilitation: Coaches provide facilitation in the learning of processes such as using instructional practices to get to desired outcomes, and they do this by focusing attention with teachers.

Coaching can also serve as an accountability measure by ensuring teachers have the support and practice needed to implement the strategies and techniques they are learning as they teach.

Peer coaching is a confidential process through which teachers share their expertise and provide one another with feedback, support, and assistance for refining present skills, learning new skills, or solving classroom-related problems (Zepeda, 2015). Much of the work in peer coaching involves classroom observations with feedback.

Typically, peer observation and peer coaching involve a cycle of a pre-observation conference, a classroom observation, and a post-observation conference with the focus of providing instructional feedback to the teacher being observed (Joyce & Showers, 1981; Zepeda, 2012, 2015). Conversations are at the heart of peer coaching. In the pre-observation conference, the coach and teacher discuss the upcoming classroom observation, selecting a focus for the observation. After the classroom observation, the coach and teacher engage in conversation about what was observed.

In a study by Wilkins, Shin, and Ainsworth (2009), participants of peer coaching shared that "receiving feedback from peers was less stressful and nonthreatening compared to being evaluated by supervisors" (p. 89). Because of the collegial nature of peer coaching, teachers believe that their peers are nonjudgmental, are supportive in their progress, and the presence of peers is less intrusive than the presence of administrators.

Peer coaching can serve to support new teachers in a variety of ways. Allison and Harbour (2009) present four main reasons that coaching should be used as a support for new teachers: (1) to encourage [novices] to discuss teaching and learning, (2) to share best practices, (3) to raise self-esteem, and (4) to encourage a "can-do" approach. Other benefits of peer coaching include:

- Teachers who receive coaching incorporate new strategies more often into their practice (Baker, 1983; Bennett, 1987).
- Coaching leads to the effective organization of instruction and improved teaching (Kohler, Crilley, Shearer, & Good, 1997; Neuman & Cunningham, 2009).
- Coaching positively improves teachers' attitudes, skill transfer, feelings of efficacy, and student achievement (Cantrell & Hughes, 2008; Cornett & Knight, 2009).

Teaching is often characterized as a lonely and isolating profession, and this is especially true for teachers at the onset of their careers. Coaching can benefit the transition from student to teacher.

## COACHING NEW TEACHERS

For the first-year teacher, the support structures in place during the student-teaching period are no longer available. Without supports, new teachers face the perils of the unknown—the responsibility for student learning. Mastering the art and science of teaching is a lifelong endeavor for those who enter and stay in the classroom. However, it is well known that a high percentage of teachers who start their careers leave shortly after the first year.

Consistently, it is estimated that between 30% and 60% of the teachers who enter their first year of teaching leave by the fifth year (Ingersoll & Strong, 2011; Pogodzinski, 2012; Pogodzinski, Youngs, Frank, & Belman, 2012). Put another way, Gray and Taie (2015) estimate that approximately one out of five teachers leave teaching during the first three years.

Without key supports led by school leaders—including principals, assistant principals, instructional coaches, and teachers—schools will continue to experience what is characterized as the revolving door where new teachers come and go. Amos for the Alliance for Excellent Education (2014) reports that teacher loss costs schools about $2.2 billion annually. But the losses go beyond the money drain, according to Wise (cited by Amos, 2014):

> The monetary cost of teacher attrition pales in comparison to the loss of human potential associated with hard-to-staff schools that disproportionately serve low-income students and students of color. In these schools, poor learning climates and low achievement often result in students—and teachers—leaving in droves. (para 2)

All school systems, but most profoundly urban and rural systems, experience the toll of losing teachers at the onset of their careers (Donaldson, 2009).

Previously in this chapter, job-embedded learning and coaching as forms of highly individualized support were examined. According to the National Commission on Teaching and America's Future (NCTAF, 2016), teachers are at the heart of the system and as such:

> We need to help our teachers stay in the profession and thrive by empowering them to develop [in] a system that is more flexible, innovative, and customized. By having more say in their professional learning, leadership roles and school culture, educators could remake their own jobs and their schools from the inside out while continually adjusting what they do based on evidence and results. (p. 5)

Darling-Hammond (2010) is resolute in her position that retaining quality teachers must become elevated as "one of the most important agendas for our nation" (p. 17). To answer this call, we must do more to support teachers as they navigate the problems of their first year, and we must be steadfast in providing supports that are differentiated to the unique and developmental needs of the newest teachers in our buildings (Zepeda, 2006, 2015). Without such supports, teacher attrition forces schools and their systems to use "band-aids to address vacant classrooms—substitutes, untrained staff, cancelled classes, larger class sizes"—all that "undermine learning" (Darling-Hammond, Sutcher, & Carver-Thomas, 2017, para 16).

Although it is not wise to generalize about the issues that any teacher, regardless of experience, goes through, there are some prevalent and recurring problems and unique situations that new teachers experience. To develop support structures, school leaders, coaches, and teacher leaders need to be aware of the range of problems new teachers experience, be able to recognize the issues within the context of the school, and then step up by providing appropriate supports and professional learning opportunities for teachers. Instructional coaches, teachers working in the formal and informal roles as peer coaches, and school leaders work in tandem to develop the newest members of the school community.

## OVERVIEW OF THE OVERALL
## ISSUES OF NEW TEACHERS

Attrition has been addressed in the prior section of this chapter. Now, attention focuses on the issues that can potentially discourage new teachers from remaining in the profession. Why do teachers leave? It's complex. The reasons why teachers leave vary and range from the stress of accountability measures such as high-stakes testing and issues related to student discipline to the profound isolation and lack of emotional support from colleagues and administrators (Boyd et al., 2011; Brown & Wynn, 2007, 2009; Ingersoll, 2012; Ingersoll & Strong, 2011).

Over time, the issues surrounding the difficulties of first-year teachers have remained constant. Problems of first-year teachers leave them feeling overwhelmed:

- With assuming responsibilities of teaching while simultaneously learning how to teach (Burkman, 2012) or what Feiman-Nemser (2012b) calls "a time of intense learning" characterized by "intense loneliness" (p. 10);
- With larger class sizes, special needs students, and extracurricular activities (Burkman, 2012);
- With differentiating instruction and motivating students (Birkeland & Feiman-Nemser, 2012)
- By unrealistic expectations (Cook, 2012; Kutsyuruba, 2012);
- With transferring theory and knowledge from college preparation programs into practical application within the classroom (Darling-Hammond, 2010; Feiman-Nemser, 2012b);
- With curriculum planning, classroom management, discipline, and working with parents (Andrews & Quinn, 2005; Veenman, 1984);
- With understanding and connecting with the culture of the school and community (Stoughton; 2007);
- By isolation (Arends & Kilcher, 2010; Goldrick, Osta, Barlin, & Burn, 2012; Ingersoll, 2012; Swanson Gehrke & McCoy, 2012);
- By accountability measures with "unprecedented challenges" (Fry & Anderson, 2011, p. 13); and
- With a lack of administrative support and collegial relationships (Boyd et al., 2011; Brown & Wynn, 2007, 2009; Swanson Gehrke & McCoy, 2012).

Professional learning for first-year teachers is paramount to not only socialize them within the school but also to indoctrinate them into the profession.

## SUPPORT FOR NEW TEACHERS

Much of the support first-year teachers receive comes in the form of induction programs, formal and informal, that may include mentoring, peer coaching, and other types of specialized professional learning opportunities. The processes of coaching were examined earlier primarily through classroom observations, feedback, and the conversations that bolster teachers reflecting about their classroom experiences. Job-embedded learning for first-years teachers would include these aspects as a way for them to learn from their work, to learn from more experienced teachers, and to learn from the students they teach.

All teachers, regardless of their experience levels, but most especially first-year teachers, need emotional support; they need to feel part of the school, and they need to feel valued from their efforts. A sense of belonging is important (Maslow, 1943). Baumeister and Leary (1995) refer to belongingness as the need for relationships that are relatively stable, ongoing, and include frequent communication. Baumeister and Leary (1995) position in their "belonginess hypothesis" that "human beings have a pervasive drive to form and maintain at least a minimum quantity of lasting, positive, and significant interpersonal relationships" (p. 497).

### Collaboration, Not Isolation

The literature is consistent in reporting that all teachers too often work in isolation (Ingersoll, 2012; Lortie, 1975). Teachers need time to work and learn from one another. Ingersoll (2012) promoted that schools and their communities must be places where "beginning teachers can learn to teach, survive, and succeed as teachers" (p. 47). Scherer (2012) tells us that "teachers want to be in environments where they are going to be successful with students, where they are getting help to do that, where they have good colleagues, [and] where they are working as a team" (p. 23).

The irony is that all teachers too often "are in their classrooms with their students with very few breaks; ... [and] the chance to interact with other adults is limited" (Cookson, 2007, p. 14). To be clear, the National Commission on Teaching and America's Future (2016), summarized:

> Teachers need regular, frequent, and structured opportunities to work together to develop curricula; design learning experiences; create assessments; devise ways to improve their individual practice; analyze student work and strategize about the best supports for specific students; help each other with questions related to content, pedagogy, or cultural competence; and share feedback. (NCTAF, 2016, p. 9)

Professional learning that is supported by coaching and its conversations can go a long way in providing job-embedded supports for all teachers.

## OVERVIEW OF CHAPTERS

The chapter authors examine professional learning that is embedded in the work of coaching. These studies included perspectives from elementary, middle, and high school teachers. The context of the schools includes rural, suburban, and urban settings. The following descriptions serve as an invitation to read the chapters that follow.

In chapter 2, Lakesha Robinson Goff explores the construction of coaching conversations by five novice teachers in a large urban area that serves a diverse population of students. The five teachers were either in their first or second year of teaching at either the elementary or secondary level. Four segments were examined (1) elements of coaching conversations, (2) common actions manifested within the confines of the coaching conversation, (3) roles of the coach, and (4) competencies and characteristics associated with novice teachers and their coaches.

The research revealed that different elements of coaching conversations exist and that specific actions taken by novice teachers and instructional coaches shaped conversations. Three themes emerged within individual cases and cross analysis: the importance of building a collegial relationship for effective coaching conversation, the ability of coaching conversations to ensure cohesiveness of the coach-teacher interaction process, and lastly the importance of a "closure" component in the coaching conversations.

In chapter 3, Angela K. Rainwater examines instructional coaches' perspectives on successes and challenges experienced while working with teachers, how instructional coaches perceive their work as they deliver job-embedded professional development in their school buildings, and the core beliefs of instructional coaches about their self-identified roles and the expectations set by principals. The school system is a rural one that enrolls 6,840 students, and the five instructional coaches provided job-embedded coaching in six of the eight elementary schools—all Title I Schools.

The results included (1) the construction of self-identified roles by instructional coaches was based on how they believed the instructional coach position should effectively serve the need of their schools, (2) the more the coaching structure aligned with the instructional coaches' strengths and beliefs of instructional coaching, the more comfortable they felt in their position, (3) obstacles such as expectations of self, content knowledge, and expert teachers could impact instructional coaches' confidence, and (4) instructional coaches gained professional credibility when they were working with teachers in their classrooms and could demonstrate understandings of instructional teaching practices.

In chapter 4, Susan Hare Bolen examines the benefits of peer observations within a learning community as an instructional support for beginning teachers. She presents their perceptions of peer observations and the learning community and examines if these types of instructional supports enhance their learning experiences.

The school system is an urban one that enrolls approximately 12,100 students. The school, designated as a Title 1, where this study took place enrolls about 517 students in grades kindergarten through fifth. The study findings reveal that participants could direct their own learning experience because they were given the opportunity and space to reflect on their learning, they worked together with their peers in a collegial setting, and they were able to enact shifts in their teaching and classroom practices.

In chapter 5, an overall analysis of the studies is offered related to the findings focusing on the processes of professional learning, the nature of job-embedded learning, and the lessons offered to school leaders to support the work of teachers.

## MOVING FORWARD

The next three chapters examine coaching. The chapter authors offer rich portrayals of what's possible in schools.

## SUGGESTED READINGS

Bambrick-Santoyo, P., & Saphier, J. (2016). *Get better faster: A 90-day plan for coaching new teachers.* Hoboken, NJ: Wiley.

Joyce, B., & Calhoun, E. (2015). *Models of professional development: A celebration of educators.* Thousand Oaks, CA: Sage Publishing.

Drago-Severson, E., & Blum-DeStefano, J. (2018). *Leading change together: Developing educator capacity within schools and systems.* Alexandria, VA: Association for Supervision and Curriculum Development.

Zepeda, S. J. (2015). *Job-embedded professional development: Support, collaboration, and learning in schools.* New York: Routledge.

Zepeda, S. J. (Ed.). (2018). *Making learning job-embedded: Cases from the field of instructional leadership.* Lanham, MD: Rowman & Littlefield.

# REFERENCES

Aguilar, E. (2013). *The art of coaching: Effective strategies for school transformation.* Hoboken, NJ: John Wiley & Sons, Inc.

Allison, S., & Harbour, M. (2009). *The coaching toolkit: A practical guide for your school.* Thousand Oaks, CA: Sage.

Amos, J. (2014). On the path to equity: Improving the effectiveness of beginning teachers. *Alliance for Excellent Education*, 14(14). Retrieved from https://all4ed. org/articles/on-the-path-to-equity-teacher-attrition-costs-united-states-up-to-2-2-billion-annually-says-new-alliance-report/

Andrews, B. D., & Quinn, R. J. (2005). The effects of mentoring on first-year teachers' perceptions of support received. *The Clearing House: A Journal of Educational Strategies, Issues and Ideas*, 78(3), 110–117. doi: https://doi. org/10.3200/TCHS.78.3.110-117

Arends, R. I., & Kilcher, A. (2010). *Teaching for student learning: Becoming an accomplished teacher.* New York: Routledge.

Baumeister, R. F., & Leary, M. R. (1995). The need to belong: Desire for interpersonal attachment as a fundamental human motivation. *Psychological Bulletin*, 117(3), 497–529. doi: http://psycnet.apa.org/doi/10.1037/0033-2909.117.3.497\

Baker, R. (1983). The contribution of coaching to transfer of training: An extension study. Ph.D. diss. Eugene, OR: University of Oregon.

Bennett, B. (1987). The effectiveness of staff development training practices: A meta-analysis. Ph.D. diss. Eugene, OR: University of Oregon.

Birkeland, S., & Feiman-Nemser, S. (2012). Helping school leaders help new teachers: A tool for transforming school-based induction. *The New Educator*, 8(2), 109–138. doi: https://doi.org/10.1080/1547688X.2012.670567

Boyd, D., Grossman, P., Ing, M., Lankford, H., Loeb, S., & Wyckoff, J. (2011). The influence of school administrators on teacher retention decisions. *American Educational Research Journal*, 48(2), 303–333. doi: https://doi.org/10.3102/0002831210380788

Brown, K. M., & Wynn, S. R. (2007). Teacher retention issues: How some principals are supporting and keeping new teachers. *Journal of School Leadership*, 17(6), 664–698. Retrieved from https://journals.rowman.com/products/authors/560359-journal-of-school-leadership/list

Brown, K. M., & Wynn, S. R. (2009). Finding, supporting, and keeping: The role of the principal in teacher retention issues. *Leadership and Policy in Schools*, 8(1), 37–63. doi: https://doi.org/10.1080/15700760701817371

Burkman, A. (2012). Preparing novice teachers for success in elementary classrooms through professional development. *Delta Kappa Gamma Bulletin*, 78(3), 23–34. Retrieved from http://www.deltakappagamma.org/NH/Spring%202012_ Professional%20Development_2-27-12.pdf

Cantrell, S., & Hughes, H. (2008). Teacher efficacy and content literacy implementation: An exploration of the effects of extended professional development with coaching. *Journal of Literacy Research*, 40(1), 95–127. doi:10.1080/10862960802070442

Cobb, P., & Jackson, K. (2011). Towards an empirically grounded theory of action for improving the quality of mathematics teaching at scale. *Mathematics Teacher Education and Development*, 13(1), 6–33. Retrieved from http://www.merga.net.au/ojs/index.php/mted/article/view/44

Cochran-Smith, M., & Lytle, S. (2009). *Inquiry as stance: Practitioner research for the next generation.* New York: Teachers College Press.

Cook, J. (2012). Examining the mentoring experience of teachers. *International Journal of Educational Leadership Preparation*, 7(1), 1–10. Retrieved from http://www.ncpeapublications.org/attachments/article/437/cook.pdf

Cookson, P. W., Jr. (2007). Supporting new teachers. *Teaching Pre-K-8*, 37(5), 14–16. Retrieved from https://search.proquest.com/docview/231938127/fulltextPDF/85B50EB9467149D2PQ/6?accountid=14537

Cornett, J., & Knight, J. (2009). Research on coaching. In J. Knight (Ed.), *Coaching: Approaches and Perspectives* (pp. 192–216). Thousand Oaks, CA: Corwin Press.

Costa, A. L., & Garmston, R. J. (2015). *Cognitive coaching: Developing self-directed leaders and learners* (3rd ed.). Lanham, MD: Rowman & Littlefield.

Croft, A., Coggshall, J. G., Dolan, M., Powers, E., & Killion, J. (2010). *Job-embedded professional development: What it is, who is responsible, and how to get it done well* [Issue brief]. Washington, DC: National Comprehensive Center for Teacher Quality.

Dana, N. F., & Yendol-Hoppey, D. (2009). *The reflective educator's guide to classroom research: Learning to teach and teaching to learn through practitioner inquiry.* Thousand Oaks, CA: Corwin Press.

Danielson, C. (2009). *Talk about teaching: Leading professional conversations.* Thousand Oaks, CA: Corwin Press.

Darling-Hammond, L. (2010). Recruiting and retaining teachers: Turning around the race to the bottom in high-need schools. *Journal of Curriculum and Instruction*, 4(1), 16–32. Retrieved from http://www.joci.ecu.edu/index.php/JoCI/article/view/41/72

Darling-Hammond, L., Hyler, M. E., & Gardner, M. (2017). *Effective teacher professional development.* Palo Alto, CA: Learning Policy Institute. Retrieved from https://webcache.googleusercontent.com/search?q=cache:hSYNgHwJx_AJ:https://learningpolicyinstitute.org/product/effective-teacher-professional-development-report+&cd=1&hl=en&ct=clnk&gl=us

Darling-Hammond, L., Sutcher, L., & Carver-Thomas, D. (2017, November 13). Why addressing teacher turnover matters. *Learning Policy Institute.* [Blog]. Retrieved from https://learningpolicyinstitute.org/blog/why-addressing-teacher-turnover-matters

Darling-Hammond, L., Wei, R. C., Andree, A., Richardson, N., & Orphanos, S. (2009). *Professional learning in the learning profession: A status report on teacher development in the United States and abroad.* Oxford, OH: National Staff Development Council.

Desimone, L. M. (2011). A primer on professional development. *Phi Delta Kappan*, 92(6), 68–71. Retrieved from http://doi.org/10.2307/25822820

Desimone, L. M., & Garet, M. S. (2015). Best practices in teachers' professional development in the United States. *Psychology, Society and Education*, 7(3), 252–263. Retrieved from www.psye.com

Donaldson, M. L. (2009). Into—and out of—city schools: The retention of teachers prepared for urban settings. *Equity & Excellence in Education*, 42(3), 347–370. doi: https://doi.org/10.1080/10665680903034753

Elementary and Secondary Education Act of 1965, Pub. L. 89-10, 79 Stat. 27, as amended by 20 U.S.C. § 6301.

Every Student Succeeds Act, Pub. L. 114-95, 129 Stat. 1802 (2015).

Feiman-Nemser, S. (2012a). *Teachers as learners.* Cambridge, MA: Harvard Education Press.

Feiman-Nemser, S. (2012b). Beyond solo teaching. *Educational Leadership*, 69(8), 10–16. Retrieved from http://www.ascd.org/publications/educational-leadership.aspx

Fry, S. W., & Anderson, H. (2011). Career changers as first-year teachers in rural schools. *Journal of Research in Rural Education*, 26(12), 1–15. Retrieved from http://jrre.vmhost.psu.edu/wp-content/uploads/2014/02/26-12.pdf

Gallwey, T. (2000). *The inner game of work.* New York: Random House.

Gray, L., & Taie, S. (2015). Public school teacher attrition and mobility in the first five years: Results from the first through fifth waves of the 2007–08 beginning teacher longitudinal study (NCES 2015-337). U.S. Department of Education. Washington, DC: National Center for Education Statistics. Retrieved from http://nces.ed.gov/pubsearch

Goldrick, L., Osta, D., Barlin, D., & Burn, J. (2012). Review of state policies on teacher induction. Santa Cruz, CA: New Teacher Center. Retrieved from https://newteachercenter.org/wp-content/uploads/brf-ntc-policy-state-teacher-induction.pdf

Hanushek, E. A., & Rivkin, S. G. (2010). Generalizations about using value-added measures of teacher quality. *American Economic Review*, 100(2), 267–271. doi: 10.1257/aer.100.2.267

Ingersoll, R., & Strong, M. (2011). The impact of induction and mentoring programs for beginning teachers: A critical review of the research. *Review of Education Research*, 81(2), 201–233. doi: https://doi.org/10.3102/0034654311403323

Ingersoll, R. M. (2012). Beginning teacher induction: What the data tell us. *Phi Delta Kappan*, 93(8), 47–51. doi: https://doi.org/10.1177/003172171209300811

Joyce, B., & Showers, B. (1980). Improving inservice training: The messages of research. *Educational Leadership*, 37(5), 379–385. Retrieved from http://www.ascd.org/publications/educational-leadership.aspx

Joyce, B., & Showers, B. (1981). Teacher training research: Working hypothesis for program design and directions for further study. Paper presented at the annual meeting of the American Educational Research Association, Los Angeles, CA.

Joyce, B., & Showers, B. (1982). The coaching of teaching. *Educational Leadership*, 40(1), 4–10. Retrieved from www.ascd.org/publications/educational-leadership.aspx

Joyce, B., & Showers, B. (1996). The evolution of peer coaching. *Educational Leadership*, 53(6), 12-16. Retrieved from http://www.ascd.org/publications/educational-leadership.aspx

Knight, J. (2005). A primer on instructional coaches. *Principal Leadership (Middle School Ed)*, 5(9), 16–21. Retrieved from http://www.principals.org/KnowledgeCenter/Publications.aspx

Knight, J. (2007). *Instructional coaching: A partnership approach to improving instruction.* Thousand Oaks, CA: Corwin Press.

Knight, J. (2008). *Coaching: Approaches and Perspectives.* Thousand Oaks, CA: Corwin Press.

Knight, J. (2011). What good coaches do. *Educational Leadership*, 69(2), 18–22. Retrieved from http://www.ascd.org/publications/educational-leadership.aspx

Knight, J. (2015). Teach to win. *Principal Leadership*, 69(2), 18–22. Retrieved from http://www.nxtbook.com/naylor/PRIK/PIK0415/index.php?startid=24#/24

Kohler, F. W., Crilley, K. M., Shearer, D. D., & Good, G. (1997). Effects of peer coaching on teacher and student outcomes. *Journal of Educational Research*, 90(4), 240–250. doi: https://doi.org/10.1080/00220671.1997.10544578

Kutsyuruba, B. (2012). Teacher induction and mentorship policies: The pan-Canadian overview. *International Journal of Mentoring and Coaching in Education*, 1(3), 235–256. doi: https://doi.org/10.1108/20466851211279484

Lortie, D. C. (1975). *Schoolteacher: A sociological study.* Chicago, IL: University of Chicago Press.

Mangin, M. M., & Dunsmore, K. (2015). How the framing of instructional coaching as a lever for systemic or individual reform influences the enactment of coaching. *Educational Administration Quarterly*, 51(2), 179–213. doi: 10.1177/0013161X14522814

Maslow, A. H. (1943). A preface to motivation theory. *Psychosomatic Medicine*, 5, 85–92.

National Commission on Teaching and America's Future. (2016). *What matters now: A new compact for teaching and learning.* Arlington, VA: National Commission on Teaching and America's Future. Retrieved from www.nctaf.org

Neuman, S., & Cunningham, L. (2009). The impact of professional development and coaching on early language and literacy instructional practices. *American Educational Research Journal*, 46(2). 532–566. doi:10.3102/0002831208328088

No Child Left Behind Act of 2001, Pub. L. 107-110, 115 Stat. 1425, as amended by 20 U.S.C. § 6301.

Pogodzinski, B. (2012). Socialization of novice teachers. *Journal of School Leadership*, 22(5), 982–1009. Retrieved from https://journals.rowman.com/products/authors/560359-journal-of-school-leadership

Pogodzinski, B., Youngs, P., Frank, K. A., & Belman, D. (2012). Administrative climate and novices' intent to remain teaching. *The Elementary School Journal*, 113(2), 252–275. doi: 10.1086/667725

Powell, D., & Diamond, K. (2013). Implementation fidelity of a coaching-based professional development program for improving head start teachers' literacy and language instruction. *Journal of Early Intervention*, 35(2), 102–128. doi: 10.1177/1053815113516678

Scherer, M. (2012). The challenges of supporting new teachers. *Educational Leadership*, 69(8), 18–23. Retrieved from http://www.ascd.org/publications/educational-leadership.aspx

Stoughton, E. H. (2007). "How will I get them to behave?": Pre-service teachers reflect on classroom management. *Teaching and Teacher Education*, 23(7), 1024–1037. doi: https://doi.org/10.1016/j.tate.2006.05.001

Swanson Gehrke, R., & McCoy, K. (2012). Designing effective induction for beginning special educators: Recommendations from a review of the literature. *The New Educator*, 8(2), 139–159. Retrieved from https://doi.org/10.1080/1547688X.2012.670571

Vanderburg, M., & Stephens, D. (2010). The impact of literacy coaches: What teachers value and how teachers change. *The Elementary School Journal*, 111(1), 141–163. doi:00135984/2010/11101-0007

Veenman, S. (1984). Perceived problems of beginning teachers. *Review of Educational Research*, 54(2), 143–178. doi: https://doi.org/10.3102/00346543054002143

Veenman, S., & Denessen, D. (2001). The coaching of teachers: Results of five training studies. *Educational Research and Evaluation*, 7(4), 385–417. doi:13803611/01/0704-385

Wilkins, E. A., Shin, E., & Ainsworth, J. (2009). The effects of peer feedback practices with elementary education teacher candidates. *Teacher Education Quarterly*, 36(2), 79–93. Retrieved from http://www.jstor.org/stable/23479253

Zepeda, S. J. (2015). *Job-embedded professional development: Support, collaboration, and learning in schools.* New York: Routledge.

Zepeda. S. J. (2012). *Staff development: What works* (2nd ed.). New York: Routledge.

Zepeda, S. J. (2018). (Ed.). *Making learning job-embedded: Cases from the field of instructional leadership.* Lanham, MD: Rowman & Littlefield.

## 2

# Staying Awake at Work: Novice Teachers and the Power of the Coaching Conversation

### Lakesha Robinson Goff

**Scenario**

Principal Dr. Patrice Brown is starting a new school year. This is her third year as a school principal and her first year in which more than half her staff of sixty-five teachers are novices. She is familiar with the district's induction program but feels strongly that she should be doing more to help support novices at the school level, especially because several novice teachers resigned last year before winter break.

Dr. Brown budgeted carefully last year to be able to hire two instructional coaches this year. To start strong, she has enrolled both coaches in the district's summer professional learning series for coaches. She went to the same training six years ago when she was an instructional coach and found it to be beneficial. Deep down though, she knows more needs to be done for her coaches as well.

Two weeks into summer, Dr. Brown sits at her desk and begins her day writing her thoughts down in her journal. She writes:

Third time's the charm they say! Well, this is year three for me! This year my novice teachers WILL BE supported and understood as individuals. They will grow professionally and help our students to be more successful than ever before. Who will lead this work? My awesome coaches ... oh yeah ... and me! WE WILL be knowledgeable and continue to become better at coaching and guiding our novices each and every day. So, what's the lingering question? It's HOW?

Key Ideas in This Chapter

- Novice teachers face various challenges when entering the profession and need job-embedded individualized support such as coaching.
- Coaching includes various activities; however, coaching conversations support novice teachers in their beginnings as professionals.
- Coaching conversations have specific components, and there are common actions that take place within each conversation.

- Coaches play various roles during coaching conversations, and there are specific competencies and characteristics that a novice and a coach must embody to ensure success.

## ABSTRACT

Coaching conversations are used to support and develop novice teachers. This chapter examines (1) the parts of a coaching conversation, (2) the common actions within a coaching conversation, (3) the roles of the coach, and (4) the novice teacher and coach competencies and characteristics.

## INTRODUCTION

The purpose of this case study was to identify the phenomena that occur within and in connection to novice teachers' coaching conversations. Although some progress has been made through the formalization of traditional and alternative teacher preparation programs, most novice teachers are still inadequately prepared for the profession upon entry (Ginsberg & Kingston, 2014) with their entrance characterized as a debilitating trial by fire (Ingersoll, 2012) where they are given the keys to their classrooms and left alone to sink or swim (Britton, Raizen, Paine, & Huntley, 2000).

With the mediated entry into the field, novices need assistance to ensure the appropriate dispositions while developing the necessary strategies and skills to be successful. Once novices enter the classroom, it is vital that they engage in a cyclical learning process in collaboration with others. Coaching is one job-embedded learning method by which school leaders can support novices. Although myriad coaching models exist, those that are effective include conversations.

Coined as a "wake-up call" by the participants in the study, the coaching conversation has matured over the years from a typical one-way exchange of technical feedback to a more nuanced and individualized experience. The coaching conversation involves a delicate balance of talking, listening, questioning, and reflecting that warrants a deeper understanding.

This study used qualitative methods to explore the following questions:

1. What are the common occurrences that emerge during coaching conversations?
2. What are novice teachers' perspectives on coaching conversations?

This chapter includes an overview of the literature, a brief context of the study, an overview of the research methods, findings, a discussion of the findings, implications for school leaders, and a summary. Discussion questions and suggested readings are also included.

## OVERVIEW OF THE LITERATURE

The literature on novice teachers, coaching, and conversation as a coaching tool is examined to identify the phenomena that occur within and in connection to novice teachers' coaching conversations.

### Novice Teachers

Novice teachers are defined as teachers in the first three years of the profession (Pogodzinski, Youngs, & Frank, 2013). Research suggests that novice teachers have become more common in schools than at any other time in the past two decades (Goldrick, Osta, Barlin, & Burn, 2012). Researchers have also highlighted new challenges for novices such as meeting accountability measures on testing mandates, implementing educational reforms, filling in curriculum gaps, and delivering student-centered instruction (Lewis, 2014; Noll & Lenhart, 2013). With the various challenges that novices face, strong support structures must be in place.

Induction, largely thought of as effective employee entry, orientation, and support programs, is a critical focus of education policy and reform designed to help novices succeed despite the challenges that they face in their beginning years in the field (Ingersoll, 2012). Induction varies by state and district but commonly includes coaching. Coaching is important, but the conversations between novices and their coaches are more important because "new teachers have things to learn, which they could not have learned before-hand ... regular and ongoing feedback around teaching and/or content standards will help guide this learning in fruitful directions" (Carver & Feiman-Nemser, 2009, p. 309).

School leaders should play a prominent role in induction by offering support, giving critical feedback, and ensuring optimal teaching and learning conditions (Brown, Benkovitz, Muttillo, & Urban, 2011). Offering support and giving critical feedback are cornerstones of coaching.

### Coaching

The current educational landscape calls for a laser focus on how to best support novice teachers to enhance their professional growth while boosting student achievement. Coaching is recognized as an effective approach toward this end. Coaching is complex and hard to define but can generally be thought of as an action-oriented change strategy that promotes growth and enhances professionalism and performance through a variety of activities and actions.

Regardless of the components, functions, and phases of coaching, "a major appeal of coaching is the opportunity to tailor information and guidance to a teacher's knowledge, skills, and specific classroom circumstances" (Powell & Diamond, 2013, p. 103). It is this individualized, differentiated, and dynamic approach to professional development that makes coaching ideal for novices.

Research describes specific components and aspects of a well-designed coaching experience. Huff, Preston, and Goldring (2013) advocate for a five-phase model that includes groundwork, assessment and feedback, goal-setting, action-planning, and ongoing assessment and support. Gardiner (2012) discusses three key factors in the experiences of novice teachers and their coaches: (1) trust as the foundation of the coaching relationship, (2) a shift in the nature of coaching from survival to sustained learning, and (3) the coach as another set of more experienced eyes helping new teachers to "see" and understand their classroom and instruction.

Interwoven throughout quality coaching experiences are coaching conversations that can serve as job-embedded learning opportunities. Coaching conversations are processes in which both the coach and the novice teacher engage in an exchange of ideas, the co-construction of knowledge, and a litany of questions, answers, and responses.

## Conversation as a Coaching Tool

Cheliotes and Reilly (2012) defined the coaching conversation as intentional and planned, focused on the other person, and situated to enhance thinking and growth to incite change that leads to action. The coaching conversation reaches beyond basic dialogue to allow novices the opportunity to broker their own success by feeling liberated, qualified, and ready to act.

The conversation itself can provide healing, promote deeper understandings by highlighting both individuals' experiences and expertise, or provide space for reflection. Heineke (2013) asserted that the coaching conversation, "gives [teachers] the opportunity to formulate ideas through speech with feedback from others to help in clarifying, questioning, and bringing together previous understandings and new learning" (p. 412).

Although coaching conversations are filled with the unexpected, the coach's overall goal is to help "facilitate the mental processes for others … to become continuous self-directed learners" (Costa, Garmston, & Zimmerman, 2014, p. 49). This study highlights coaching conversations and novice teachers' perspectives about them.

## CONTEXT OF STUDY

This case study took place in a large urban area with five novice teachers. The novice teachers (Alexandria Martin, Rachel Copeland, Erica Lindsey, Stephanie Roberts, and Monica Greene—all pseudonyms) were in their first or second year of teaching at either the elementary or secondary level.

## RESEARCH METHODS

Each participant was interviewed twice, totaling ten semi-structured interviews. The first interview was used to establish rapport and to gather firsthand accounts of novices' experiences related to their conversations with their coaches. The second interview helped to clarify individual perspectives shared in the first interview, garner feedback on initial findings, examine certain trends, capture any lingering thoughts, and ask additional questions of the participants. Participants were asked to respond to one open-ended journal prompt.

Because multiple data sources were used and collection took place simultaneously with analysis, the constant comparative method of data analysis was used to provide an in-depth understanding of the phenomena that occurred within and in connection to novice teachers' coaching conversations (Corbin & Strauss, 2008; Glaser & Strauss, 1967). During the process of coding, data began to merge into larger and smaller units. From these units, trends in the data began to emerge.

A cross case analysis with each novice as an individual case revealed the distinct parts of a coaching conversation, common actions within coaching conversations, roles of the coach, and novice teacher and coach competencies and characteristics.

## FINDINGS

The common occurrences that emerged during coaching conversations are separated into two distinct areas: the building blocks of coaching conversations and actions taken within coaching conversations.

### The Building Blocks: Parts of a Coaching Conversation

Although coaching conversations were flexible and organic, the participants identified five main parts of coaching conversations: observation,

self-assessment, feedback, planning and practicing, and summary. Figure 2.1
outlines the five distinct components of a coaching conversation as identified
by the novices.

An *observation* is a prerequisite for any coaching conversation. Rachel
stated, "You have to observe first to see what I do. After that observation, we
actually have some things to talk about." Observations are vehicles by which
to ground conversations. Observations also provided coaches with substantial
information to ensure that coaching conversations were purposeful.

*Self-assessment* is an element of coaching conversations in which the
novices' voice takes center stage. Novices shared their own opinions and
thoughts on the observation, their strengths and weaknesses, and even
personal challenges that made it difficult to be successful in the classroom.
Most participants enjoyed being able to voice their opinions. Erica shared,
"I like to say how I feel first before the feedback." By having novices self-
assess before hearing feedback, coaches put themselves in a prime position
to affirm, take note of self-described areas of opportunity, and to understand
further the novices' perspectives and experiences.

*Feedback* must be at the heart of all conversations and should always be
"balanced." Novices described feedback as "grows and glows," "strengths
and weaknesses," "the poop sandwich," "flames and focus," and "good and
bad." Coaches should be intentional when giving feedback, ensuring that they
discuss strengths and what teachers need to work on for future observations.

After feedback, coaching conversations continue with a *planning and
practicing* component. Planning and practicing take place in a variety of
ways, varying from goal setting to actual modeling and role-playing activities. The goal of the planning and practicing component is clarity. Novices
voiced the need to be clear on what actions should be taken to strengthen
their classroom practices. Stephanie shared, "I need to be able to answer the
questions "What next?" and "How?"

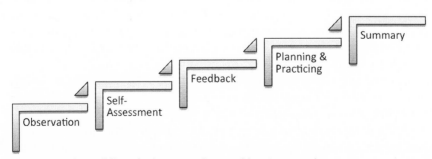

**Figure 2.1   The Building Blocks: Parts of a Coaching Conversation**

The *summary* component takes place at the end of the conversation and brings closure to the conversation. Alexandria's summary included "quiet time" in which she and her coach reflected on the conversation and next steps. Erica's summary centered on her assistant principal's one question, "What can I do to help you?"

To come to closure, Monica shared that her coach did a written recap that served as a "checklist" and "daily reminder" of what she needed to focus on next. Novices enjoy bringing closure to each coaching conversation and routinely use the summary segment as a check for understanding as well as to prioritize next steps to move forward.

## The Balancing Act: Actions within a Coaching Conversation

There are two distinct areas of action within a coaching conversation: novice moves and coach moves. Novice moves are defined as actions taken by novices with little to no prompting by the coach. Coach moves are intentional actions taken by coaches to direct the conversation and to support the novice on a path of self-discovery.

There are four common novice actions: building context and understanding, sharing anecdotes, articulating strengths and areas of opportunity, and envisioning the future.

*Building context and understanding* is a novice move that builds trust and sets the stage for collaboration. Novices take time during coaching conversations to paint a clear and vivid picture of their unique situation and environment. Even though coaches and novices might work in the same school building, novices are the "experts on [their] experiences," and their perspectives provide great insight. Coaches have an opportunity to garner a deep understanding of a novice's experience as the novice shares his or her perspective on school initiatives, district mandates, classroom occurrences, individual students, and parent interactions.

*Sharing anecdotes* is a significant action that novice teachers engage in during coaching conversations. Taking on the role of storyteller, each anecdote is typically "descriptive, detailed, and purposeful." Many stories are celebratory, whereas others are told to unveil issues, garner ideas, or showcase progress. Each anecdote provides the coach with another glimpse into the novice's world.

Novices deemed coaching conversations as safe spaces for *articulating strengths and weaknesses*. Novices typically articulated a "mix" of both strengths and weaknesses during a coaching conversation. However, participants repeatedly warned that novices often become fixated on their weaknesses. When novices were driven by their weaknesses, it was the coach's job to highlight strengths that could be leveraged to steer the conversation in a more positive direction.

Participants revealed that *envisioning the future* was an enjoyable and integral part of coaching conversations. At times, the future for some novices was the very next day or week. Monica shared, "[Tomorrow] I'm going to be walking around and checking in with students. I'm going to throw in a few wrong problems just so I can make sure they are with me."

Other novices focused on the end of a semester or school year. Alexandria's vision was concise yet long term as she explained, "I want them to feel like they learned something. I want them to go into next year knowing that they are prepared." A novice's vision is a source of inspiration and motivation that coaches should artfully build upon.

There are three common coach actions: affirming, sharing expertise, and exploring through inquiry.

*Affirming* allows coaches to build novices' confidence and competence. At a basic level, affirmation takes place in the form of direct and specific praise. During Rachel's coaching conversation, her coach declared, "You are really, really great at seeing those non-verbal cues from students when they don't understand. We can use that strength to build." Coaches can also affirm by naming best practices that the novice is using successfully or take time to legitimize a novice's feelings.

*Sharing expertise* was a natural part of many coaching conversations. Given their wealth of knowledge and experiences, it is acceptable for coaches to share their expertise with novice teachers during coaching conversations; however, they must do so in a respectful manner that does not downplay the novices' own expertise. Coaches should feel comfortable sharing their own personal experiences in the classroom, offering suggestions and ideas, or using previous coaching experiences with the novice to move the conversation toward a specific destination.

*Exploring through inquiry* was a key component in every coaching conversation. Inquiry allowed coaches to be guides and to ensure that novices were building the skill and capacity needed to be professional and effective. One novice shared that "all of the questions help me to really think and examine what I do."

Novices revealed that coaches even embedded inquiry into their feedback. First sharing their feedback and then asking questions such as, "How could we put an assessment strategy in place that allows every student the opportunity to process and participate?" or "What do they do that lets you know that they respect you?" By using mostly open questions, coaches encouraged novices to think, reflect, envision, and act.

Figure 2.2 highlights the actions taken within a coaching conversation by novices and coaches.

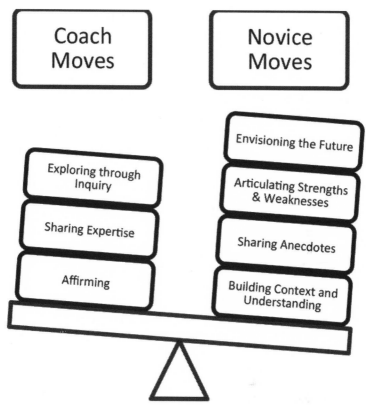

Figure 2.2   The Balancing Act: Actions Within a Coaching Conversation

Novice teachers' perspectives on coaching conversations centered on two categories: roles of the coach and novice teacher and coach competencies and characteristics.

## Roles of the Coach

Novice teacher participants identified several roles that coaches play during coaching conversations. As the novices explained each role in detail, two distinct coaching roles emerged: coach as consultant and coach as trusted adviser.

The coach as consultant role focused on teaching and learning. It also highlighted the coach's willingness to share knowledge openly with the novice. Novices saw this role as one that recognized the coaching relationship as "not a leader and a follower thing but a meet in the middle type of thing."

**Table 2.1. Participants' Perspectives on the Roles of the Coach**

| Coach as Consultant Descriptors | Coach as Trusted Adviser Descriptors |
| --- | --- |
| • Expert | • Colleague |
| • Guru | • Mentor |
| • Consultant | • Friend |
| • Third Eye | • Therapist |
| • Alternate Set of Eyes | • Big Sister |
| • Guide | • Sounding Board |

Alexandria relayed, "Giving me the answers isn't really coaching." Coaches must work "alongside" novices asking "guiding questions."

The coach as trusted adviser role was more intimate in nature. Rachel shared, "[Coaches] know you more intimately because they're helping you become better." In the role of trusted adviser, a coach often focused on challenges that were taking place outside of the classroom that were adversely affecting the classroom experience. In this role, the coach actively listened, offered support, and shared new perspectives.

Table 2.1 summarizes the novices' perspectives on the roles coaches play during coaching conversations.

## Novice Teacher and Coach Competencies and Characteristics

There are two common characteristics that both novices and coaches exhibit: a positive disposition toward coaching and a high level of engagement. Additionally, novices bring a sense of ownership, and coaches bring an ability to "steer the ship." Four out of the five novice teacher participants shared that a positive disposition toward coaching "sets the stage" for a successful coaching conversation.

Although novices and coaches differ related to what actions they took within a conversation, they had to be open to the coaching relationship, which involved having a sense of curiosity and a willingness to take risks. Rachel focused on curiosity sharing that it was important for novices to have "questions for your coach." Erica and Stephanie revealed that coaches must be equally as curious and ask questions like, "What can I do to help you?" and "What are your goals?"

A willingness to take risks is also paramount. Novices and coaches must exhibit extreme levels of flexibility, courage, and humility that allow them to be open to new experiences and new ways of thinking. Monica believed that novices had to be "humble enough to try something." Alexandria reflected, "As a coach, sure … you were a first-year teacher but probably ages ago.

Things are different, so you have to be open to doing things differently." If teachers are taking risks, coaches must follow suit.

A high level of engagement is an additional characteristic that both the coach and the novice embody. A high level of engagement was categorized by investment, vulnerability, trust, and authenticity. When these four characteristics were present novices felt that they were in a "committed" coaching relationship.

The novices and coaches were invested if they saw themselves as partners with one goal, which was to increase student achievement. Erica divulged that when coaches are invested, "They understand you … what you're about and what you're trying to accomplish." Alexandria, Monica, Erica, and Rachel shared that novices showed their investment by being "active participants," and understanding that "coaching is a process that you have to just stick with."

Vulnerability, trust, and authenticity were ways to heighten the level of engagement for both parties. Alexandria viewed vulnerability as the ability to, "open up to other people telling me my faults," while Stephanie likened it to "penetrating walls." Monica and Stephanie shared that trust was of equal value and that novices had to, "Trust the person that you're talking to. Trust the advice that they're giving you." However, Rachel and Erica revealed that this trust could only be given if novices felt "understood." Rachel voiced, "I can only trust once I know you are not judging me."

Authenticity stems from trust. Monica warned novices to avoid "trying to make yourself sound and look good." Stephanie explained the need "to be off" around her coach which meant that she did not have to put on any airs in her coach's presence and that she could be true to who she was and exactly what was going on in her classroom. To that end, novices also wanted coaches to feel comfortable being "exactly who they are." Rachel advised coaches to, "Just be yourself … that's when you will be at your best."

Although novices and coaches shared vital common characteristics, there was one characteristic that participants indicated specifically applied to novices. A sense of ownership was necessary for the novices, often characterized by an acute awareness of the shared responsibility in a coaching relationship along with the novice's creation of a distinct classroom vision. When novices brought a sense of ownership with them to the coaching conversations, they positioned themselves as knowledgeable and active participants who had a unique destination in mind.

The coaches' ability to "steer the ship" in the appropriate direction is a characteristic that only applies to coaches. Coaches should see the "whole picture" and guide novices toward the most fruitful destination. To do so, coaches must discern, prioritize, and make decisions.

**Table 2.2. Necessary Characteristics and Competencies of Both Parties**

| Positive Disposition towards Coaching Descriptors | High Level of Engagement Descriptors |
| --- | --- |
| • Openness to relationship<br>• Willingness to be coached<br>• Sense of curiosity<br>• Willingness to take risks<br>• Wanting to learn and grow | • Investment<br>• Vulnerability<br>• Trust<br>• Authenticity<br>• Team/Partnership<br>• Active Participation<br>• One Goal |

**Table 2.3. Necessary Characteristics and Competencies of Each Individual Party**

| Sense of Ownership Descriptors<br>Novices Only | Ability to Steer the Ship Descriptors<br>Coaches Only |
| --- | --- |
| • Awareness<br>• Shared responsibility<br>• Professionalism<br>• Vision | • Discernment<br>• Strength<br>• Ability to prioritize<br>• Ability to make decisions |

Novices' minds were constantly "spinning," and at times they needed their coaches to determine "what need[s] to be done tomorrow versus next week." Novices revealed that coaches were viewed as individuals that could move their classrooms in the direction they needed to go by funneling actions and activities into a hierarchy. To do so, coaches had to be confident in their ability to "pinpoint what things … need to be worked on" and to make a "final decision when needed."

Table 2.2 outlines the competencies and characteristics that both the novice and the coach must embody and the descriptors used by participants. Table 2.3 outlines the independent competencies and characteristics that novice teachers and coaches must have and the descriptors used to define them.

## DISCUSSION OF FINDINGS

Three unique themes emerged within the data of the individual cases and the cross case analysis. The three themes are:

1. A collegial relationship is a prerequisite for effective coaching conversations.
2. Coaching conversations are the connective tissue of coaching.

3. Novice teachers view closure as a critical component of coaching conversations.

Theme 1: *A collegial relationship is a prerequisite for effective coaching conversations.*

A collegial relationship is one in which the authority, power, and responsibility are shared equally between the coach and the novice teacher. Trust and equality are core components of a collegial relationship. Monica, Stephanie, and Erica named trust directly as one of the most important things that novices must exemplify. Erica stated, "The conversation is where that personal thing comes in. There needs to be a certain level of trust between you and the coach." Equality was also of value as novices described their coach as a colleague, teammate, or peer. Shared responsibility and authority honored the novices' knowledge and previous personal and professional experiences.

Novice participants also highlighted the impact of the initial interactions with their coach. Alexandria shared that when she met her coach for the first time they "didn't really even talk that much about teaching but about who we were as people." Erica described her first encounter with her coach as "relaxing and fun." The initial interactions between the coach and the novice were key in determining the overall feel and tone of the relationship. These interactions focused on who the novices were inside and outside the classroom and what they hoped to achieve.

Theme 2: *Coaching conversations are the connective tissue of coaching.*

With the variety of activities that coaching encompasses, the coaching conversation served as the connective tissue that ensured that the entire process was cohesive. Coaches helped teachers to build understanding and to make connections through playing various roles in and outside conversations, using inquiry, and breaking conventional coaching boundaries.

Coaches played an assortment of roles including those of sounding board, big sister, consultant, mentor, friend, good cop, bad cop, and therapist. Stephanie shared that coaches needed to know how to "break out" of different roles, and Monica noted that coaches needed to know "who to be and when."

Inquiry was a critical piece of effective coaching conversations. A coaches' ability to ask powerful and intentional questions allowed the novice to have a voice in the conversations. Participants revealed that when coaches were "curious," the conversations were "rich" and "a lot of learning [takes] place." Participants also noted a feeling of "professionalism" and "accomplishment," when they could figure things out "alongside" their coach.

Participants revealed that coaching conversations are not to be restrictive. Coaching conversations happen anywhere, anytime, and with anyone. Novices agreed that coaching conversations were more effective when they happened face to face, but sometimes less conventional methods were of value. Participants noted that effective coaching conversations took place on the phone, in Google hangout, via e-mail, and even through a series of text messages.

Theme 3: *Novice teachers view closure as a critical component of coaching conversations.*
Participants placed high value on "constructive criticism" and being able to "practice stuff [to] get it right." However, participants noted the critical need for closure at the end of each conversation to summarize the overall experience and to ensure that their needs were met. Most participants discussed the final segment of each coaching conversation as a "summary" or "closing."

Novices stressed the importance of taking time to review topics discussed and proposed actions before ending the coaching conversation. Rachel urged coaches to even, "[e]nd the conversation with a follow-up email or a summary of the conversation" to give novices something "tangible." Although little research has been done on bringing closure to coaching conversations, the findings revealed that providing time to summarize what has been discussed and what actions should follow helped to "check for understanding" and hold novices "accountable [for] what was discussed."

Offering the appropriate support and ensuring mutual satisfaction are two additional elements that bring closure to coaching conversations. The participants reported that their coaches often asked questions such as, "What can I do to help you?" or "What resources do you need to be successful?" Monica shared, "[Coach] never walks away without knowing what I need." Participants also highlighted the importance of coaches closing out each conversation by making sure that novices' needs have been met. Alexandria advised coaches to ask novices, "Did you get what you needed out of the conversation?"

## IMPLICATIONS FOR SCHOOL LEADERS

This study reinforces the idea that coaching inclusive of coaching conversations is a quality job-embedded learning opportunity that helps to support and develop novice teachers. School leaders play an integral role in ensuring that coaching is of high quality. There are four overarching implications for school leaders.

1. Novice teachers need job-embedded individualized support and guidance in the form of coaching.

2. Coaches need ongoing professional development around coaching with a focus on coaching conversations.
3. Scheduling must include time and space for novice teachers and their coaches to engage in coaching conversations.
4. School leaders must see themselves as coaches.

Novice teachers represent a unique population in schools and are faced with distinct challenges that set them apart from other staff members. Leaders must be fully aware of this distinction and provide job-embedded support that is tailored to each novice's specific needs. Coaching is a research-based method that easily allows for individualization and growth.

Coaches are the driving force behind coaching. Coaches often receive training at the beginning of the school year and are left to their own devices for the remainder of the year. Leadership must provide ongoing professional development so that coaches can continuously hone their craft, particularly around the art of coaching conversations. At a basic level, coaches should have a common understanding of the building blocks of coaching conversations.

Even the most qualified coach will not be effective without space and time. It should not be the job of the novice or coach to find time for coaching conversations. Although participants agreed that other methods like Google Hangout allow one-on-one conversations to happen in a nontraditional way, traditional face-to-face conversations are still preferred. School leaders must intentionally plan the coaches' and novices' schedules to allow the appropriate time and space for coaching conversations. In doing so, the school leader places a high value on coaching that is clear to both the novice and the coach.

In many cases, novices' initial interactions are with school leadership during the interview process. In turn, novices view leadership as the instructional compass for the school early on and are eager for their feedback and guidance. School leaders should see themselves as coaches and make every effort to establish collegial relationships with novices early. Additional professional development around coaching could be effective for leadership, particularly around the distinction between coaching and evaluation.

## SUMMARY

This research affirms that coaching is a multifaceted job-embedded approach to provide novice teachers with the support they need during their induction years. Although coaches and novices participate in several activities including, co-planning, modeling, and co-teaching, the coaching conversation connects the dots and makes the overall practice cohesive.

The value of coaching conversations is directly related to the quality of the relationship between the coach and the novice. A collegial relationship is paramount, and without it, no coaching can take place. Starting with the initial interaction, a coach and novice must build trust and establish equality. When coaches and novices sit down at the "coaching table," each must be cognizant of what they are bringing to the conversation.

A positive disposition and a high level of engagement are vital for both parties. However, novices must also bring a sense of ownership, and coaches must feel comfortable and competent enough to "direct the ship." Both parties must be committed and invested for the relationship and subsequently the conversation to bear fruit.

Additionally, novices live in a busy world and their jobs as teachers are vast and often all encompassing. Bringing closure to each coaching conversation helps novices to review what has been discussed and check for their own understanding related to next steps. It also allows them to share any lingering thoughts or concerns and ensure that their needs have been met. With time being a precious commodity, ensuring understanding and satisfaction at the end of each coaching conversation is key.

Time has also impacted how novices view coaching conversations. Participants revealed that coaching conversations happen at anytime, anywhere, and with anyone. Coaching conversations are breaking conventional boundaries, and novices are appreciative of the innovations that are increasing coaches' accessibility and considering convenience and practicality.

The idea of coaching as a practice to support and develop novice teachers is not a novel one. However, the power and potential behind every coaching conversation is emerging as a key lever of effective practice. Coaching conversations are not casual dialogues where the coach holds all the power. Instead, they are organic discussions in which the novice's voice is appreciated and respected.

As the population of novice teachers continues to grow in our nation's schools, the field of education itself has a responsibility to provide novices with an induction experience that is holistic and effective. Coaching is one route that can guide teachers toward self-sufficiency and student success. The roles of a coach and the activities that they involve themselves in are vast. However, no activity can take the place of the coaching conversation.

Decades ago we called for novice teachers to come out of their silos and to connect with their colleagues and communities. Novice teachers came out, but coaching activities to a large degree did not. No longer can coaching activities exist in isolation. The coaching conversation is the key to intimately and intentionally connect the practice of coaching so that novice teachers are nestled in an interconnected system built to individually help them grow, develop, and excel.

## Discussion Questions

1. As a school leader, reflect on the current practices used to support and develop novice teachers. What practices should be continued? What practices should be eliminated? What practices should be added?
2. Initial interactions, trust, and equality are important to the foundation of a collegial relationship. How can you plan for effective initial interactions with novices? What are some activities that can help establish trust and equality early on?
3. Some school leaders experience difficulty assuming a coaching role. How do you plan to balance the dual nature of your role as an evaluator and coach such that your coaching conversations are still of value?

## SUGGESTED READINGS

Drago-Severson, E., & Blum-DeStefano, J. (2016). *Tell me so I can hear you: Developmental approach to feedback for educators*. Cambridge, MA: Harvard Education Press.

Gardiner, W. (2012). Coaches' and new urban teachers' perceptions of induction coaching: Time, trust, and accelerated learning curves. *The Teacher Educator*, 47(3), 195–215. doi: 10.1080/08878730.2012.685797

Huff, J., Preston, C., & Goldring, E. (2013). Implementation of a coaching program for school principals: Evaluating coaches' strategies and the results. *Educational Management, Administration and Leadership*, 41(4), 504–526. doi:10.1177/1741143213485467

Heineke, S. F. (2013). Coaching discourse: Supporting teachers' professional learning. *The Elementary School Journal*, 113(3), 409–433. doi: 0013-5984/2013/11303-0005

## REFERENCES

Britton, E., Raizen, S., Paine, L., & Huntley, M. A. (2000). *More swimming, less sinking: Perspectives on teacher induction in the U.S. and abroad*. Paper presented at a meeting of The National Commission on Teaching Mathematics and Science in the 21st century. Paper retrieved from http://web.WestEd.org/online_pubs/teacherinduction/index.html

Brown, K. M., Benkovitz, J. B, Muttillo, A. J., & Urban, T. (2011). Leading schools of excellence and equity: Documenting effective strategies in closing achievement gaps. *Teachers College Record*, 113(1), 57–96. Retrieved from www.tcrecord.org

Carver, C., & Feiman-Nemser, S. (2009). Using policy to improve teacher induction: Critical elements and missing pieces. *Educational Policy*, 23(2), 295–328. doi: 10.1177/0895904807310036

Cheliotes, L. G., & Reilly, M. F. (2012). *Opening the door to coaching conversations.* Thousand Oaks, CA: Corwin.

Corbin, J., & Strauss, A. (2008). *Basics of qualitative research: Techniques and procedures for developing grounded theory* (3rd ed.). London: Sage.

Costa, A. L., Garmston, R. J., & Zimmerman, D. P. (2014). *Cognitive capital: Investing in teacher quality.* New York: Teachers College Press.

Gardiner, W. (2012). Coaches' and new urban teachers' perceptions of induction coaching: Time, trust, and accelerated learning curves. *The Teacher Educator*, 47(3), 195–215. doi: 10.1080/08878730.2012.685797

Ginsberg, R., & Kingston, N. (2014). Caught in a vise: The challenges facing teacher preparation in an era of accountability. *Teachers College Record*, 116(1), 1–48. Retrieved from http://www.tcrecord.org

Glaser, B., & Strauss, A. (1967). *The discovery of grounded theory.* Chicago, IL: Aldine.

Goldrick, L., Osta, D., Barlin, D., & Burn, J. (2012*). Review of state policies on teacher induction.* Santa Cruz, CA: New Teacher Center. Retrieved from www. newteachercenter.org

Heineke, S. (2013). Coaching discourse: Supporting teachers' professional learning. *The Elementary School Journal*, 113(3), 409–433. doi:0013-5984/2013/11303-0005

Huff, J., Preston, C., & Goldring, E. (2013). Implementation of a coaching program for school principals: Evaluating coaches' strategies and the results. *Educational Management, Administration and Leadership*, 41(4), 504–526. doi: 10.1177/1741143213485467

Ingersoll, R. M. (2012). Beginning teacher induction: What the data tell us. *Phi Delta Kappan*, 93(8), 47–51. Retrieved from www.pdkintl.org/publications/kappan

Lewis, G. M. (2014). Implementing a reform-oriented pedagogy: Challenges for novice secondary mathematics teachers. *Mathematics Education Research Journal*, 26(2), 399–419.doi:10.1007/s13394-013-0092-5

Noll, B. L., & Lenhart, L. A. (2013). Meeting first-year challenges in reading instruction, *The Reading Teacher*, 67(4). 264–268. doi: 10.1002/trtr.1214

Pogodzinski, B., Youngs, P., & Frank, K.A. (2013). Collegial climate and novice teachers' intent to remain teaching. *American Journal of Education*, 120(1), 27–54. doi: 0195-6744/2013/12001-0002

Powell, D. R., & Diamond, K. E. (2013). Implementation fidelity of a coaching-based professional development program for improving head start teachers' literacy and language instruction. *Journal of Early Intervention*, 35(2), 102–128. doi: 10.1177/1053815113516678

*3*

# Instructional Coaches' Perspectives: Successes and Challenges Experienced While Working with Teachers

## Angela K. Rainwater

**Scenario**

It is 8:30 A.M. and Betty is late for an instructional coach meeting. The principal is out of the building, so Betty is called to the front office to talk with a parent who has concerns about an incident that happened in her child's classroom the day before. Although she is the instructional coach, Betty has administrative duties because there is no assistant principal employed at her school.

When Betty finally walks into the school's media center for her meeting, a teacher starts a conversation about a need in her classroom pertaining to teaching resources. Betty has the resources in her office, but she apologizes to the teacher for having to rush off for another meeting. Betty makes a note to remind herself to take the resources to the teacher immediately after the meeting.

During the meeting, Betty has a tough time focusing because she is thinking about what is needed from her that day—administrative duties, classroom observations, co-teaching, and a coaching session. To another instructional coach, this type of schedule could cause tension toward the school administration, but for Betty, this is what she believes should be done for the students and the success of her school. She enjoys holding a position that is multifaceted and is willing to do what is needed in the defined role as instructional coach at her particular school.

Key Ideas in This Chapter

- Instructional coaches' roles differ from school to school based on the needs of the school.
- Although they face barriers in their work, instructional coaches feel comfortable in their position when the coaching structure aligns with strengths and beliefs about instructional coaching.

• Instructional coaches maintain credibility by understanding the work of classroom teachers and teaching students.

## ABSTRACT

This chapter explores (1) the perspectives of instructional coaches related to the successes and challenges they experience while working with teachers; (2) how instructional coaches perceive their work providing job-embedded professional development; and (3) the beliefs of instructional coaches related to their self-identified roles and expectations from school principals.

## INTRODUCTION

For many years, a frontline debate of educational policy has been the quality of education that students receive in schools in the United States. Policy efforts such as the No Child Left Behind Act (2001) and the federal Race to the Top (2009) competition have recognized the urgency of employing and supporting quality teachers. The Every Student Succeeds Act of 2015 is explicit in its definition of professional learning and the importance of coaching as a support.

Credentials are necessary to obtain a teaching position, but more importantly, "[t]he lynchpin to improving teacher quality and seeing gains in student achievement rests, in part, to the overall professional development made available to teachers" (Zepeda, 2012, p. 6). The positive connection between educational outcomes, teacher quality, teacher effectiveness, and professional development is that professional learning is imperative to teacher and student success.

A common component for teacher support in the professional-development literature includes instructional coaching. The ongoing interest in coaching emerged, in part, from the intersection of rising expectations for student achievement, research indicating the strong relationship between teacher quality and effectiveness and student achievement, and a new paradigm for teacher learning.

Professional learning, supported by a coach, allows teachers to reflect on their teaching practices and to strengthen their pedagogical beliefs about effective teaching (Joyce & Showers, 1996; Knight, 2007). In a study conducted by Coburn and Woulfin (2012), it was noted that teachers were more likely to make substantial changes in their classroom practice when they learned from a coach about skills related to content rather than from other sources such as school leaders and system administrators. In an additional study, Elder and Padover (2011) indicated a 95 percent implementation rate of new practices when coaching was provided.

Coaching is a focal point in the Every Student Succeeds Act (2015) that calls for sustained, job-embedded, data-driven professional learning for teachers and leaders. Instructional coaches are now a mainstay in most schools, and therefore it is important to explore the perspectives of instructional coaches related to the successes and challenges they experience while working with teachers. From such an exploration emerges a deeper understanding of how school leaders can support the efforts of instructional coaches and the professional learning they provide for teachers.

## OVERVIEW OF THE LITERATURE

Instructional coaching is a model developed through research related to the inclusion of added supports to extend professional development for teachers (Knight, 2005, 2009). Instructional coaches' focus on supporting teachers do their daily work as a means to improve teaching practice (Knight, 2005). Research shows that effective coaching can promote teachers' effective implementation of curriculum reform and new teaching practices (Bruce & Ross, 2008; Knight, 2005) and moreover, Knight (2011) believes that, "next to the principal, coaches are the most crucial change agent in a school" and goes on to say that "good coaching gets results—and it gets them fairly quickly" (p. 50).

## THE INSTRUCTIONAL COACH MODEL

The school system in the study employs an instructional coach in all eight elementary schools in the district. To frame the coaching program, the work by Knight (2007) and his book *Instructional Coaching: A Partnership Approach to Improving Instruction* was used as a guide. The Big Four framework organizes interventions and provides focus for the work of coaches (Knight, 2007).

The Big Four areas include: (1) teacher and student behavior; (2) content knowledge; (3) direct instruction; and (4) formative assessment. Knight's (2011) coaching model is built on a partnership approach where "a partnership is about shared learning as much as it is about shared power" (p. 20).

## Benefits of Instructional Coaching

Instructional coaching requires dedication, persistence, and meaningful collaboration with all involved in the coaching process. When highly qualified instructional coaches are in place to support teachers using the right teaching methods and the partnership approach, improvement can happen (Knight, 2011). Researchers at the Kansas University Center for Research on Learning (KU-CRL), directed by Knight (2005), studied instructional coaches who worked with Kansas University's Pathways to Success and Maryland's Department of Special Education's Passport to Success. The research suggests that there are three primary reasons why coaching should be included within school improvement initiatives.

First, when conditions are right, coaching leads to implementation of effective teaching practices. In the projects, implementation rates were consistent at 85 percent with well-constructed coaching programs. Second, Knight (2005, 2011) found that with the consistent support from a coach, teachers' fidelity to implement proven instructional practices increases. Third, the research shows coaching promotes positive conversations in schools. When coaches provide support to teachers and take the lead in starting positive conversations, teachers benefit.

## Cautions within Instructional Coaching

Research by Knight (2005) underscores the importance of effective coaching, and he cautions that if the principal and instructional coach do not work together in partnership, professional learning can be negatively impacted. Principals and instructional coaches need to build a relationship where both work together clarify the work of the coach, identify teachers who will receive services from the instructional coach, and the types of professional development needed to focus on school improvement. Knight (2011) cautions that the principal and instructional coach must be careful to work together in partnership to reduce teacher resistance to new programs and interventions.

## THE INSTRUCTIONAL COACH

An instructional coach, as defined by Knight (2005), is "an on-site professional developer who teaches educators how to use proven teaching methods" (p. 17). Coaches collaborate with teachers to identify practices that will effectively address needs and help teachers implement those practices and any newly learned skills (Knight, 2005). Together, the teacher and coach set goals and develop a plan to meet those goals with the purpose of improving teachers' instructional practices for increased student learning (Oliver, 2007).

When a coach works with a teacher, the work is directly related to the job of the teacher, occurs during the day while on the job, and should take into consideration the experience, maturity, knowledge, and career path of the teacher (Zepeda, 2015). Instructional coaches engage teachers in various professional development activities that include, for example, modeling effective teaching practices, observing teaching practices, discussing effective teaching, and providing feedback (Knight, 2007).

## Characteristics of Effective Instructional Coaches

Although research saturates the professional-development arena, many providers of staff development do not possess the knowledge base and skills needed to support teachers in reform efforts (Hill, 2009). Similarly, studies have found that the fidelity with which coaches implemented workshops was no greater than that of their teachers in implementation of classroom practices (Powell & Diamond, 2013).

Studies have drawn attention to the characteristics coaches must possess to lead professional development opportunities that effectively foster new understandings and learning of content and pedagogy, and promote a collegial atmosphere. Key areas include subject-specific content and pedagogy and communication skills (Knight, 2007; Saphier & West, 2010).

## Content and Pedagogy

It is critical that coaches are content specialists who have the ability to support teachers in deeper understanding and the use of the content that leads to improved practice (Kinkead, 2007). Further, coaches need to have a thorough understanding of how children learn so they can pass on to teachers the most appropriate and effective pedagogical strategies that data analysis indicates is needed and support teachers in implementing those strategies in their own teaching practices (Kowal & Steiner, 2007; Pomerantz & Pierce, 2013). Having the knowledge of content and pedagogy is only a starting point for an instructional coach. Effective communication and interpersonal skills are imperative to impart content and pedagogical knowledge.

## Communication and Interpersonal Skills

As part of effective communication and interpersonal skills, coaches must be capable of creating opportunities for conversations about classroom practices and facilitating learning opportunities that support teachers in transforming their practices. Coaches who use effective communication and interpersonal skills are attuned to teacher needs and are able to make necessary adjustments to address and support particular needs within the classroom (Mangin & Dunsmore, 2015).

Effective coaches must be able to create an atmosphere of open and safe learning for adults (Knight, 2007). According to research regarding coaching and communication, effective coaches actively listened, built trusting relationships, fostered safe learning environments, communicated effectively with school personnel, employed reflective questioning strategies, and provided constructive feedback for improvement (Knight, 2009; Mangin & Dunsmore, 2015). An instructional coach may have content and curriculum expertise, but without effective interpersonal and communication skills, professional-development efforts will result in ineffective outcomes (Knight, 2009).

Communication skills are needed not only to build relationships that foster an effective working environment between teachers and coaches, but also to foster effective learning environments for teachers. Instructional coaches should develop communication strategies that focus on facilitating teachers' reflective thinking (Mangin & Dunsmore, 2015). By using communication skills to foster reflection, instructional coaches can guide teachers toward self-directed learning and problem solving.

Employing a coach without expertise in the areas of content and pedagogy and communication and interpersonal skills dissipates improvement efforts and results in professional learning that is ineffective for the purpose of instructional improvement. The job of a coach is important to meet the needs of teachers who in turn can meet the needs of students entrusted to their care (Knight, 2005; Zepeda, 2015).

## CONTEXT OF THE STUDY

The purpose of this study was to examine how instructional coaches perceived their work with teachers as they provided job-embedded professional development in their schools. The single research question that guided the study was: *What are instructional coaches' perspectives about the successes and challenges they experience while working with teachers?*

The research site is located in a rural area of the United States. The school district operates fourteen schools and employs approximately 668 teachers who serve about 6,840 students. The schools in the district include eight elementary schools, three middle schools, one ninth-grade academy, one high school, and a Success Academy. The eight elementary schools are Title 1, and enrollment ranges from approximately two hundred to six hundred students.

Participants in the study are instructional coaches who serve six of the elementary schools. One instructional coach is half-time, serving two different schools.

## RESEARCH METHODS

The researcher recruited and then chose the participants through purposeful sampling (Patton, 2002) and using criteria: the coaches had to have at least three years of instructional coaching experience in the school system and hold at minimum a Master's degree. Five instructional coaches—all white females—(Betty, Heather, Marsha, Suzanne, and Sonya—all pseudonyms) met the criteria for the study and agreed to participate.

The research design included semi-structured interviews and journal entries as the primary methods of data collection. The instructional coaches were interviewed twice, with follow-up questions being asked via e-mail in addition to the interviews. The participants were asked to keep a journal to record their thoughts, experiences, and emotions regarding coaching sessions with teachers. Various documents such as coaching letters and e-mails between coaches and teachers were collected to triangulate the data. During the process of the study, a researcher's journal was also kept to document thoughts, questions, concerns, and reflections about being in the field with the instructional coaches.

The constant comparative method was used to analyze the data. The constant comparative method assures that data are systematically compared to all other data in the set (Corbin & Strauss, 2008). For example, interview data were compared not only with other interview data, but also with data from journal entries, documents, and the researcher's notes. As codes and categories developed, the researcher gained clarity on instructional coaches' perspectives while also allowing for the development of the overarching themes.

## FINDINGS

What are instructional coaches' perspectives about the successes and challenges they experienced while working with teachers? The findings that evolved during the study span three areas: (1) differing duties among instructional coaches; (2) confidence within the job; and (3) credibility within the instructional coach position. When data across the participants were examined, four themes emerged.

Theme 1: *Instructional coaches self-identify their roles based on their beliefs about how the instructional coach position should meet the needs within their respective schools.*

It is important to consider the instructional coaches' perspectives of their role. Within the case, instructional coaches have differing duties, which is expressed as being beneficial to the teachers in the school district. The duties of the instructional coach depend on the needs within each school. Heather shared, "Every principal in every building has their own expectation of what this role is."

Data revealed that each coach was comfortable in the expectations from their individual principals, and in some cases, instructional coaches indicated they would not be able to work for a principal who had expectations that did not align with their personal beliefs about the purpose of the instructional coach role. Heather shared that she would not be comfortable as an instructional coach with the expectation of assuming administrative duties. She felt strongly enough about the role of an instructional coach focusing on instruction that if offered the position in a school where administrative duties were the expectation, she would choose to be a classroom teacher.

Suzanne also shared that her focus was not on administrative duties and that she would decline being an instructional coach if administrative duties became a requirement. Table 3.1 provides an overview of the differing approaches and structures to coaching found across the instructional coaches' schools.

In addition to differing duties among the instructional coaches, each coach also identified roles for themselves. The self-identified roles were linked to the personal belief each coach had about the job of an instructional coach and the confidence each had within the job. Table 3.2 provides the self-identified roles the instructional coaches assumed within the school district.

Marsha's role of partnership is in the form of providing for teachers when they need assistance, such as in taking students to lunch, watching students on the playground, and teaching a class. Marsha spent time developing relationships on a personal level. She believed an important characteristic in her role was to give teachers someone to talk to when there were struggles and "wished coaching cycles were more of a priority."

Within her coaching duties, Sonya believed there was a line between what she called "light coaching" and "heavy coaching." She considered "light coaching" to be helping with copies and small duties of the like to get to know teachers and to build a relationship. Sonya shared that it was important to wean herself off those duties as a coach to get to the important "heavy coaching" of focusing on professional development and instruction.

Although Suzanne was an instructional coach, she continued to identify herself as a teacher. Suzanne used her "teacher's heart" to create a positive

**Table 3.1. Approaches to and Structures for Coaching**

| Coach | Coaching Approaches and Structures |
|---|---|
| Betty | • Plans for and provides professional development at both schools<br>• Works with all stakeholders<br>• Works with small groups of students if needed<br>• Teachers' needs drive the daily schedule<br>• Acts as administrator when needed |
| Heather | • Provider of professional development<br>• Works with administrators to plan professional development<br>• Teacher of small groups of students<br>• Feels the need to be close to the classroom so not to lose sight of what it is like to be a teacher<br>• No administrative duties |
| Suzanne | • Member of instructional team with school administrators<br>• Facilitator of professional development<br>• Mentors teachers to be coaches |
| Marsha | • Provider of professional development<br>• Organizes schoolwide assessments and data from the assessments<br>• Leader of grade-level data discussions<br>• Leader, mentor, and counselor for teachers instructionally and socially<br>• Freedom from administration to plan with and assist teachers in problem solving |
| Sonya | • Provider of professional development<br>• Analyzes data and guides teachers in reflection on data<br>• Plans with administrators for grade-level and teacher goals |

coaching structure for professional development in her school. She worked with teachers to find their strengths and then taught those teachers how to share their strength by coaching and mentoring other teachers. For Suzanne, this structure alleviated the stress of having to be "a guru" in all areas while using other teachers as experts, which was an area that has affected the confidence of other instructional coaches.

Within Suzanne's school, the variety of teachers' strengths has become a great resource for learning. The identified strengths were used in creating learning groups of teachers within the school for professional development. It was important to allow opportunities for teachers to learn from each other, which was accomplished by teachers being provided times to visit and observe classrooms of teachers who were identified as having strengths in their area

**Table 3.2. Instructional Coaches' Self-identified Roles**

| Coach | Self-Identified Roles |
|---|---|
| Betty | "I'm on call when an administrator is needed."<br>"My role is multi-faceted."<br>"Whatever I need to do to make our school successful is what I do." |
| Heather | "My bottom line is about teaching and learning in the building. I feel like the main purpose of school is the instruction."<br>"I feel a little more able to be a coach to these teachers because I still teach kids everyday." |
| Suzanne | "I have a teacher's heart."<br>"I feel I am called to mentor and teach teachers, find their strengths, and help them to coach and mentor other teachers." |
| Marsha | "I am here to inspire and serve teachers. I think service above yourself is the phrase I would use."<br>I am a leader, mentor, and counselor both instructionally and socially." |
| Sonya | "I have to be sort of a chameleon. I have to be able to adapt quickly to needs in the building." |

of interest. By doing this, an open collaborative atmosphere of teachers as learners and leaders was created, and professional growth is fostered.

Theme 2: *Instructional coaches feel comfortable in their position when the coaching structure framed by the school's principal aligns with their strengths and beliefs of instructional coaching.*

The participants shared they had positive relationships with their principals, and they worked with their principals to set and carry out plans to meet professional-development goals in the school. In relation to Knight's (2005) practice of the principal and instructional coach being in agreement on how the instructional coach implements interventions within the school, Suzanne discussed a particular time when she and her principal planned how to incorporate the use of a new book to support reading strategies.

The principal stated to Suzanne, "We're not going to hand out that book for teachers to have. Before it goes out, we need to have a plan." Further, the principal asked Suzanne, "What do you think we need to do? I think we need a little bit more planning together so we can all decide what [the strategies] look like and that we are clear on what we want."

Marsha shared that her principal trusted her enough to give her opportunities to make decisions at times. When Marsha was making certain decisions she bounced ideas off the principal and asked, "What do you think about this?" or "Is this a good time to roll this out?"

When identifying teachers who would work with the instructional coach, all participants shared they worked collaboratively to identify teachers. Suzanne explained that the principal was in the classrooms frequently and noticed particular needs of teachers. The principal would bring the need to Suzanne's attention; if the need was noticed during an evaluation, the principal asked the teacher to seek assistance from Suzanne while also notifying Suzanne of the need.

Sonya shared that the meetings she had with her principal were important. She elaborated that "We have weekly meetings. We talk about expectations. We talk about instructional areas we need to work on, together as a team, keeping our focus unified on the same things." Sonya also shared that she and her principal learned early on that they had to work "to be on the same page; otherwise, they risked giving teachers mixed messages."

If Suzanne noticed a teacher who needed support, she sought advice from the principal about how to approach the teacher. Suzanne also discussed that she and the principal brought to each other's attention teachers who excelled in a particular area. They would talk with those teachers about modeling or mentoring other teachers. In their coaching structure, the coach not only supported teachers who needed assistance, but she also worked to develop teachers who could give assistance to others.

The participants spoke of the necessity work alongside their principals to support curricular reforms and to deal with teachers who were resistant to modifying instructional or assessment strategies. Heather and Sonya discussed approaching administration about a teacher or teachers being unwilling to incorporate a practice. In both instances, the administrators and instructional coach together decided how to handle the situation.

In Heather's case, it was decided that she would continue to offer assistance to the grade level of teachers who needed to incorporate guided reading into their instruction, but she found many excuses as to why it was not happening. In Sonya's case, the teacher adamantly refused to incorporate the new initiative. In that particular case, it was decided by Sonya and the principal together, that Sonya would not continue to approach the teacher regarding support.

Participants shared details about the positive relationships with their principals and the shared belief of the professional environment in their respective schools as a positive aspect of their positions. Heather and Suzanne additionally shared that they would want to be in the classroom as a teacher if their beliefs about the instructional coach position and their principal's beliefs about the instructional coach position were not in alignment.

Theme 3: *Barriers such as expectations of self, content knowledge, and other teachers affect instructional coaches' confidence within the job.*
When discussing successes and challenges of their personal effectiveness and feelings about the job, the instructional coaches in this study focused on being critical of their performance and shared concerns of having a lack of confidence in their job at times.

## Barriers

Although all participants had more than 10 years of experience as classroom teachers before becoming an instructional coach and all had served as an instructional coach for more than three years, they spoke about being uncomfortable in certain situations. The instructional coaches identified barriers that affected their job performance. Most barriers were not within control of the participants.

A barrier for Betty was traveling between two schools and not always being able to have face-to-face time with teachers when needed. When teachers were not able to have her support as needed, Betty tried to make it better by staying positive. Although the positive attitude helped Betty in building relationships with teachers, she still felt the weight of not being at a particular school when needed, which affected her confidence in her job.

Having an "infectious personality" also helped Heather when dealing with the barrier of new initiatives. Heather explained that she felt "frustrated" by the lack of information sharing about what was happening between her school and information sources external to the school site, especially around end-of-year standardized testing. She was getting information about testing requirements and changes at the last minute.

Although there was nothing Heather could do to remedy her frustration, she felt responsible for the teachers' overwhelmed feelings. Heather was able to be positive with the teachers and bring perspective to them about the situation, which corroborates research by Knight (2007) in relation to how an "infectious personality" is beneficial in calming a difficult situation.

Marsha explained that when the new student learning standards were to be implemented, she received backlash from teachers and had to carry the load alone of trying to get the teachers on board. In Marsha's school during this time, the lack of involvement by the principal could have played a role in teachers' resistance to the new standards and the negative impact that resistance had on the professional-development sessions.

Suzanne encountered teachers whose strong personalities created barriers. She explained that a grade level of teachers in her school had strong personalities, which created tension. Because of the tension, she rarely worked with that grade level; however, one of the team members was a strong teacher, and Suzanne worked with her as a teacher leader to spread ideas within that team.

Collectively, the coaches identified three barriers that negatively affected their confidence: (a) expectations of self; (b) content knowledge; and (c) teachers as experts.

## Expectations of Self

Findings indicated that instructional coaches' expectations for themselves impacted the confidence they feel about the job. For example, Betty stated that she felt like a failure when she could not "save" a teacher she was coaching. The coached teacher would not make an independent effort to implement effective strategies after being coached as was indicated in a directive from the principal. This teacher ultimately ended up leaving education.

Suzanne shared it was her personality trait of being sensitive that caused her to question her ability to be the best person for the instructional coach position. Suzanne explained that when she heard great ideas or new problem-solving strategies from others she wondered, "Why didn't I think of that?" At other times, Suzanne was afraid of making a mistake for fear of losing credibility with teachers. Instances such as these caused Suzanne to feel incompetent, and she shared, "You know, that's just my personality. It works great for me in some in some senses. But in others, it does not."

Similarly, Marsha and Heather felt overly responsible for success in their respective schools. Marsha became "stressed out" by trying to make sure she was doing everything possible to meet the needs of all staff members. She felt the weight of responsibility of students and teachers failing because of her lack of knowledge. Heather felt responsible for many layers of the school, even being concerned about why a teacher may be frustrated or why a teacher may choose a certain resource when a better one was available.

## Content Knowledge

Findings indicate that the participants believed it was not possible for instructional coaches to be content specialists in all areas. Sonya shared that having both a math and a literacy coach would be more beneficial for teachers because typically one person cannot be an expert in both areas. Sonya felt that her area of weakness was fifth-grade math. Betty also felt her area of weakness was math in general, sharing, "I try to be [good in math] and I can fake it, but math is not my strength."

Suzanne felt more competent in math, whereas Marsha felt she was not as competent as she would like to be in any area. Betty specifically mentioned that she needed more professional development in the area of math. She

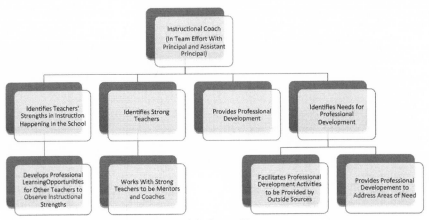

Figure 3.1   Learning Community Model of Coaching

stated, "As far as professional development, more math would be helpful for me." Suzanne explained, "It's all about instructional strategies and keeping up. We have to be one step ahead. [Professional learning for coaches] is all about instructional strategies."

## Teachers as Experts

Suzanne and Sonya believed that because no one person is a "guru" in all areas, relying on strong teachers was vital for implementing new strategies. Because Suzanne was not comfortable with fifth-grade math content and pedagogy, she relied on the fifth-grade math teachers to work together with her on new initiatives.

Suzanne created a learning community model at her school. The professional learning model helped to develop strong teachers as mentors and coaches for their peers. The professional learning tapped into the strengths within the school and combined instructional coaching with peer coaching. Figure 3.1 illustrates the learning community model of coaching that Suzanne developed in her school.

Theme 4: *Instructional coaches maintain credibility of the instructional coach position by understanding the job of a classroom teacher and teaching students.*

Findings indicated that the participants maintained credibility of their position by their complete understanding of the job of a classroom teacher. Heather stated, "If you're too far removed from the classroom, it's hard to have credibility with teachers and it's hard to connect with them." Additionally, Heather shared that an instructional coach has to understand all the moving parts within the duties of a classroom teacher and to consider these parts when planning professional development.

Marsha explained that instructional coaches must be involved with what teachers were being asked to do from all levels—district, state, and federal. Marsha shared that she needed to know more about her teachers, so she could address any hurdles that could get in the way of meeting goals. Suzanne believed that if she was vulnerable and teachers could see her go through struggles as they do, her role as a coach became stronger.

In addition to understanding the job of a classroom teacher, data indicated that instructional coaches believed they maintained credibility with teachers by also teaching students. Heather stated, "Instructional coaches still work with students an awful lot so they don't lose sight of how hard the work is." Suzanne shared that it was important for instructional coaches to know the "ins and outs" of teaching strategies. Sonya believed that going into classrooms and teaching students provided opportunities for teachers to reach out to her for additional supports.

## DISCUSSION OF FINDINGS

Instructional coaches' self-identified roles are grounded in their personal beliefs about instructional coaching. The themes presented were connected to the instructional coaches' perspectives, and they were guided by each coach's personal beliefs about the work of an instructional coach. Instructional coaches' self-identified roles begin with the personal belief of each coach. Confidence and maintaining credibility are affected by the self-identified role. Figure 3.2 demonstrates the connection of instructional coaches' personal beliefs, self-identified roles, confidence with the work, and maintaining credibility.

## IMPLICATIONS FOR SCHOOL LEADERS

School leadership is responsible for the professional growth that occurs in their schools, and much of what happens in schools is based on the culture that the principal and other people create. Understanding instructional coaches' perspectives helps principals to create a deeper understanding for framing professional development and to create a school atmosphere that leads to teacher learning and more effective classroom instruction.

When principals and instructional coaches work together to establish professional development for their schools, instructional coaches' perspectives about the coaching structure should be taken into consideration to address any

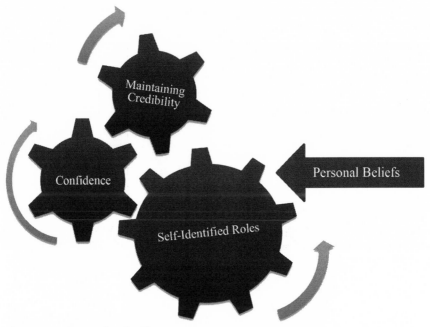

**Figure 3.2   Connecting the Themes**

concerns and gaps that may be created by self-identified roles. For example, a coach who spends a lot of time fulfilling surface needs such as finding resources, making photocopies of work, and taking over the class to allow a break for the teacher, may not be able to spend the necessary amount of time planning and conducting needed professional development.

Practitioners who are leaders of instructional coaches within a district must take steps to ensure that coaching structures in schools are implemented in an effective fashion. Leaders must support the premise that the purpose of an instructional coach is to be, among many other things, an on-site professional developer who teaches educators how to use evidence-based teaching practices and supports them in applying these practices in their classrooms. In the end, the structures that support coaches being able to attend to the individual and collective learning at the site is dependent on the principal who sets the direction of these types of efforts.

## SUMMARY

This study builds on the existing research base of effective instructional coaching by examining the perspectives instructional coaches hold about working with teachers. On the surface, certain coaching strategies lead to effective professional development; however, the self-identified roles of instructional coaches and the coaching structure established in a school also have an effect on professional development.

Beliefs about the role one holds about being an instructional coach affect practice. Instructional coaches' self-identified roles are grounded in their personal beliefs about instructional coaching and affect their performance in working with teachers. It is important for school leaders and instructional coaches to discuss their beliefs about their roles that will evolve based on practices. Having a unified team framing professional learning in a school will go a long way in supporting an atmosphere focused on job-embedded learning that promotes teacher growth and development.

### Discussion Questions

1. What is the instructional coach's role within the school? Does that role align with the instructional coach's personal beliefs regarding the work?
2. How do the instructional coach's personal beliefs impact work with teachers and school leaders?
3. Are there barriers preventing the instructional coach from meeting the goals set by school leadership? How can those barriers be overcome?

## SUGGESTED READINGS

Aguilar, E. (2013). *The art of coaching: Effective strategies for school transformation.* San Francisco: Jossey-Bass.

Fullan, M., & Knight, J. (2011). Coaches as system leaders. *Educational Leadership,* 69(2), 50–53. Retrieved from http://www.ascd.org/publications/educational-leadership.aspx

Zepeda, S. J. (2015). *Job-embedded professional development: Support, collaboration, and learning in schools.* New York: Routledge.

## REFERENCES

Bruce, C., & Ross, J. (2008). A model for increasing reform implementation and teacher efficacy: Teacher peer coaching in grades 3 and 6 mathematics. *Canadian*

*Journal of Education*, 31(2), 346–370. Retrieved from http://www.jstor.org/stable/20466705

Coburn, C. E., & Woulfin, S. L. (2012). Reading coaches and the relationship between policy and practice. *Reading Research Quarterly*, 47(1), 5–30. doi:10.1002/RRQ.008

Corbin, J. W., & Strauss, A. L. (2008). *Basics of qualitative research* (3rd ed.). Thousand Oaks, CA: Sage.

Elder, D. L., & Padover, W. (2011). Coaching as a methodology to build professional practice. *Journal of Research in Innovative Teaching*, 4(1), 138–144. Retrieved from http://www.nu.edu

Every Student Succeeds Act, Pub. L. No. 114-95 (2015).

Hill, H. C. (2009). Fixing teacher professional development. *Phi Delta Kappan*, 90(7), 470–477. Retrieved from http://www.pdkintl.org/publications/pubshome.htm

Joyce, B., & Showers, B. (1996). The evolution of peer coaching. *Educational Leadership*, 53(6), 12–16. Retrieved from http://www.ascd.org/publications/educational-leadership.aspx

Kinkead, S. (2007). *Improving instruction through coaching*. Silverdale, WA: Center for Strengthening the Teaching Profession.

Knight, J. (2005). A primer on instructional coaches. *Principal Leadership*, 5(9), 16–21. Retrieved from http://www.nassp.org

Knight, J. (2007). *Instructional coaching: A partnership approach to improving instruction*. Thousand Oaks, CA: Sage.

Knight, J. (2009). Coaching: The key to translating research into practice lies in continuous job-embedded learning with ongoing support. *Journal of Staff Development*, 30(1), 18–22. Retrieved from http://www.nsdc.org

Knight, J. (2011). What good coaches do. *Educational Leadership*, 69(2), 18–22. Retrieved from http://www.ascd.org/publications/educational-leadership.aspx

Kowal, J., & Steiner, L. (2007). *Instructional Coaching*. (Issue Brief). Washington, DC: Retrieved from http://files.eric.ed.gov/fulltext/ED499253.pdf

Mangin, M. M., & Dunsmore, K. (2015). How the framing of instructional coaching as a lever for systemic or individual reform influences the enactment of coaching. *Educational Administration Quarterly*, 51(2), 179–213. doi:10.1177/0013161X14522814

No Child Left Behind Act of 2001, Pub. L. No. 107-110, 115 Stat. 1425 (2002).

Oliver, B. (2007). Send me in coach. *Just ASK Publications & Professional Development*, 4(9). Retrieved from http://www.justaskpublications.com

Patton, M. Q. (2002). *Qualitative research and evaluation methods* (3rd ed.). Thousand Oaks, CA: Sage.

Pomerantz, F., & Pierce, M. (2013). When do we get to read? Reading instruction and literacy coaching in a failed urban elementary school. *Reading Improvement*, 50(3), 101–117. Retrieved from https://www.highbeam.com/doc/1G1-347001443.html

Powell, D. R., & Diamond, K. (2013). Implementation fidelity of a coaching-based professional development program for improving head start teachers' literacy and language instruction. *Journal of Early Intervention*, 35(2), 102–128. doi:10.1177/1053815113516678

Saphier, J., & West, L. (2010). How coaches can maximize student learning. *Phi Delta Kappan*, 91(4), 46–50. Retrieved from http://pdkintl.org/publications/kappan/

US Department of Education. (2009). *Race to the top executive summary*. Retrieved from http://www2.ed.gov/programs/racetothetop/executive-summary.pdf

Zepeda, S. J. (2012). *Professional development: What works* (2nd ed.). New York: Routledge.

Zepeda, S. J. (2015). *Job-embedded professional development: Support, collaboration, and learning in schools*. New York: Routledge.

*4*

# Meaningful Job-Embedded Professional Learning for Beginning Teachers

## Susan Hare Bolen

**Scenario**

*Excerpt from a November Learning Community Meeting:*
  Catherine shared that she was "struggling with reaching a student." While trying to help Catherine figure out strategies to address the behavioral issues of the student, Adam asked her, "What kind of behavior are you seeing from him? Do you know why he is doing these inappropriate behaviors?" Then Adam explained what he understands about why students misbehave. Adam then offered to observe the student in Catherine's room. This classroom observation focused on understanding and solving a problem of practice.

Key Ideas in This Chapter

1. Beginning teachers do desire frequent, intentional time to collaborate.
2. Peer observations within learning communities provide high-quality job-embedded instructional support for beginning teachers.
3. Shifts in instruction are a realistic expectation after meaningful professional learning experiences.

## ABSTRACT

This chapter explores (1) what happens when peer observation within a learning community structure serves as an instructional support for beginning teachers; (2) what beginning teachers think about peer observation and learning community; and (3) if these types of support make a difference for them.

## INTRODUCTION

Beginning teachers need an infusion of knowledge with opportunities to integrate what is learned through the support that professional development can offer (Ingersoll & Strong, 2011; Kardos & Johnson, 2010). Consequently, it is key that beginning teachers are socialized into the profession by being immersed into a culture of lifelong learning that is cohesive, supportive, questions the tasks of teaching, and provides instructional support (Bickmore & Bickmore, 2010; Wong, 2002).

This study explored what happened when peer observation within a learning community structure served as an instructional support for beginning teachers. The research sought to understand what beginning teachers think about peer observation and learning community and if these types of support make a difference for them.

Learning community in this study was defined as a group of first-, second-, and third-year teachers who met monthly with their instructional coach to reflect and write about their peer-observation experiences, share their learning with the community members, and talk through their next steps. Journal writing related to peer-observation experiences, and perspectives about those experiences served as the opening activity at each of these community meetings. The meetings were held in a learning community member's classroom.

The instructional coach served as facilitator setting agendas and sending reminders of meeting dates and times. This sharing allowed the learning community to work interdependently toward individual goals that permitted and enhanced personal and professional growth. The configuration of this learning community allowed teachers to talk about questions that were important to them and to build collegial relationships that were grounded in practice, fostered teacher development, and raised teacher capacity.

This chapter offers an overview of the literature, the context of the study, the research methods, and the findings. The chapter concludes with a discussion of the findings that include implications for school leaders.

## OVERVIEW OF THE LITERATURE

The literature on professional development, beginning teachers, peer observation, and learning communities is presented to give background information for and context to this study.

## Professional Learning

Professional development is optimal when there is understanding about how adults learn, what motivates adults, the work environment of the school, and the characteristics of the teaching profession (Zepeda, 2012, 2015). Knowledge of how teachers grow, what their needs and interests are, and respect for their profession should all be reflected in the professional-development opportunities made available to teachers (Glickman, Gordon, & Ross-Gordon, 2017; Zepeda, 2017). Successful professional development builds both individual and organizational capacity while simultaneously focusing effort on supporting student learning (Gordon, 2016).

Effective professional development is focused on contextual issues and implementing instructional changes that improve student learning. Intentional professional development begins with a clear purpose and worthwhile goals. Ongoing, systemic professional development is continuous, takes advantage of daily job-embedded opportunities for learning, and involves everyone that influences student learning (Guskey, 2000; Zepeda, 2012). When professional development becomes a daily, ongoing learning experience customized to meet the needs of teachers, it has become job embedded (Zepeda, 2015).

Learning that is relevant, promotes collegiality, enhances reflection, combats isolation, and provides timely feedback to participants facilitates the transfer of new skills into practice (Joyce & Showers, 1995; Zepeda 2012, 2015). Professional development is highly contextualized when it is designed according to the varying needs, developmental levels, expertise, and commitment of teachers (Glickman et al., 2017).

## Beginning Teachers and Their Supports

To reduce attrition among beginning teachers whose preparation paths are diverse, we need to understand their challenges and to identify support systems (Ingersoll, 2012; Parker, Ndoye, & Imig, 2009). First-year teachers are "expected to be expert and independent from the start" (Kardos & Johnson, 2010, p. 2085). This expectation often leads teachers to leave the profession at high rates (DeAngelis & Presley, 2011; Goldring, Taie, & Riddles, 2014). Findings from research about the problems first-year teachers encounter paint consistent patterns that range from classroom discipline, curriculum planning, and motivating students to insufficient support from school administrators and completing required paperwork (He & Cooper, 2011; Veenman, 1984).

In a study of first- and second-year teachers in six school districts, Gilbert (2005) found that peer observation, mentoring, instructional feedback, common planning time, and having smaller classes were what new teachers indicated as giving them the most instructional support. Teachers explicitly stated they "wanted multiple opportunities to interact with their more experienced colleagues while doing meaningful work" (Gilbert, 2005, p. 39). New teachers value collegial work, desire opportunities to work in a learning community, and consider positive interactions with their peers an essential part of their work (Meanwell & Kleiner, 2014; Mee & Haverback, 2014).

Specifically, new teachers want structured time for planning, preparation, and professional development (National Commission on Teaching and America's Future, 2003, 2005). Therefore, instructional supports for beginning teachers must be reevaluated and restructured because beginning teachers' professional needs, their school-based supports, and retention are all linked to long-term success (DeNeve & Devos, 2017).

## Peer Observation

Peer observation is a form of job-embedded professional development that supports teachers learning from each other (Gordon, 2016; Zepeda, 2015). The purpose of peer observation is to improve the quality of teaching and learning via feedback and conversations based on practice and reflection. A clear, well-communicated focus built on common purpose is essential for laying the foundation of trust necessary to make peer observation effective (Miranda, 2012). The peer observation design is a threefold process that includes (1) pre-observation meeting, (2) classroom observation, and (3) post-observation session.

New teachers need time to observe and to get feedback from colleagues while practicing their craft (Joftus & Maddox-Dolan, 2002). When new teachers are provided the opportunity to observe their peers and to be observed, they

- develop understandings of different perspectives,
- learn to listen for and try out new ways of knowing,
- participate in discussions of effective classroom practice,
- make decisions related to curriculum, and
- connect their practice to instructional improvement (Grossman, Wineburg, & Woolworth, 2000; Johnson, Berg, & Donaldson, 2005).

Peer observation has many benefits. First, peer observation is a useful, learner-driven tool. New staff members gain tremendously from seeing good practice in action, and veteran teachers often receive validation related to the implementation of classroom practices. Second, peer observation enhances the overall professional-development program of the school by helping to shift the culture to one of learning for all, removing barriers to observing classroom strategies in context, and elevating analysis and reflection to job-embedded status. Finally, peer observation promotes reflective dialogue that can support changes in practice (Fiszer, 2004; Hammersley-Fletcher & Orsmond, 2004).

Most new teachers have few opportunities to observe the work of their peers. Moreover, most teachers are rarely observed by anyone other than their students or evaluator (Fiszer, 2004). Typically, teachers do not have the opportunity to observe a peer, have a collegial conversation, and get feedback related to sharpening their instructional practices (Fiszer, 2004). Therefore, additional inquiry that links opportunities for beginning teachers to partici-pate in peer observation in a learning community setting is timely.

## Learning Communities

Learning communities build capacity. A learning community can be the catalyst for powerful job-embedded learning focused on improving instruc-tion in all classrooms by giving teachers multiple opportunities to learn new methods, apply them, and observe positive results within the context of a community. Participation in a learning community can serve to connect faculties, build strong teaching practices, and focus on the goals of the school (DuFour & Eaker, 1998; Harris & Jones, 2010). Moreover, under the right conditions, learning communities raise teacher effectiveness, stu-dent achievement, teacher efficacy, and job satisfaction (Gordon, 2016; Katzenmeyer & Moller, 2009).

The learning community developed at Godwin Elementary School (GES), the site where the present research was conducted, focused on building a collaborative environment for beginning teachers to come together and learn by examining practices. The learning community met formally one time per month for about two hours to engage in sharing concerns, troubleshooting solutions, and discussions about teaching and learning.

## CONTEXT OF THE STUDY

The data collected are from one elementary school, GES, in one school dis-trict (pseudonym). The Shepherd School District (SSD, pseudonym) is an urban system that employs approximately 975 teachers with an enrollment of 12,100 students in fourteen elementary schools, four middle schools, two high schools, and one alternative school. Fifty-four percent of the students are black, 19% white, 20% Hispanic, and 2% Asian. All students in the SSD receive a free or reduced-cost lunch and breakfast.

GES has 517 students in pre-kindergarten through fifth grade. The racial breakdown of the students is 53.2% black, 29.2% white, 12.7% Hispanic, and 4.9% Asian. Fourteen percent of the students are enrolled in special education, and 5% are enrolled in the English for Speakers of Other Languages (ESOL) program. The school faculty includes twenty-four classroom teachers, eighteen support teachers, one counselor, one instructional coach, and two administrators.

## RESEARCH METHODS

This study included six beginning teachers who were part of a learning community at GES. Case study methods were chosen to understand the perspectives of the six participants, and the theoretical framework of constructivism was used to understand how they made sense of peer observation within a learning community setting as an instructional support.

Data sources included two semi-structured interviews with each of the six participants, observation of the participants during the two-hour monthly learning community meetings, the participants' journal entries (approximately three per month), field notes from the interviews and the observations made during the learning community meetings.

Data analysis occurred concurrently with data collection (Merriam & Tisdell, 2015; Ragin & Becker, 1992). All interviews were audio recorded and transcribed. After the first interview, questions and responses were analyzed, and the second set of interview questions was formed. The researcher listened to the audio recordings and read the transcriptions noting and coding data that linked back to beginning teachers' perspectives about peer observation and learning communities. Notations were made in the margins of the transcripts and coded. Categories were formed and compared with other data.

Data were further analyzed using the constant comparative method (Glaser & Strauss, 1967). The basic strategy was to compare constantly beginning with a particular data bit and comparing it with other data bits in the set (Merriam & Tisdell, 2015). In this study, data bits from individual interviews, learning community notes, and field notes were compared with each other to determine categories within each case. Then case-based categories were compared across cases.

### Overview of the Participants

This study was limited to first-, second-, and third-year teachers. Overall, information about the six teachers who participated in this study is in Table 4.1.

**Table 4.1. Participant Profiles**

| Participant | Gender | Teacher Preparation Experience | Number of Years in Teaching | Number of Years at the School | Job Assignment |
|---|---|---|---|---|---|
| Ginny | Female | BS, four-year traditional program | 3 | 3 | First-grade classroom |
| Beth | Female | MEd, BA in History | 1 | 1 | Second-grade classroom |
| Catherine | Female | BS, four-year traditional program | 1 | 1 | Second-grade classroom |
| Denise | Female | BS, four-year traditional program | 3 | 3 | Third-grade classroom |
| Adam | Male | BS, four-year traditional program | 3 | 5 | Fourth-grade Special Education (collaboration and direct instruction) |
| Edward | Male | Master's in Psychology, alternative certification program | 2 | 2 | Fifth-grade classroom |

# FINDINGS

In writing the findings, the researcher endeavored to help the reader hear the voices of the participants and to understand the participants' perspectives about what they were learning. The data were distilled through cross-case analysis yielding three major propositions.

Proposition 1: *Beginning Teachers Can Be Self-Directed in Their Own Professional Learning.*
The participants valued choice within their peer-observation experiences. They used words like *pertinent, relevant,* and *motivating* to explain what giving them choice did for their peer-observation experience. Catherine voiced the idea that peer observations based on her needs and her decisions "put me in charge of my own learning." Beth mentioned "if you give them

[teachers] some choice ... they're more invested in it, and I think they get more from it." Furthermore, Edward felt that "having choices in what you are observing gives you an opportunity to engage in something ... that applies to your instruction." The ability to choose was empowering to the participants.

Adam stated that choice and school culture made peer observations powerful. The school site has a culture that respects teachers as professionals and trusts them to work in a professional manner. Therefore, providing peer-observation experiences that were built on teacher choice was a natural fit. By giving teachers the space to make their own professional learning decisions, teachers were in effect being told, "I believe that you can do this, and I believe that you will do this." This speaks to their ability to solve their own dilemma and to have the initiative to follow through.

By positioning choice in the peer-observation process, problem posing and problem solving were the norm. Teachers were given permission to voice problems and to pose questions of practice around those problems. In the learning community meetings, participants referenced language centered on problem posing and questions of practice as they shared what they were learning through their peer-observation experience.

Phrases like "I have been struggling with," and "so my question is" were common. By empowering teachers to shape their own professional learning, teachers were given permission to not know the answers to their questions. In the words of Denise, "I'm not the only one that doesn't know what is going on all of the time."

Furthermore, this sense of autonomy has shaped these beginning teachers into lifelong learners and problem solvers. Adam believes "it's a learning process being a teacher." Edward said that he now realizes "teaching is a constantly changing profession because it directly deals with the human behavior of learning."

The teachers were able to articulate what they were learning individually and during learning community sessions. The participants spoke of change and shifts in practice after each peer observation. This problem solving, learner mentality is reflected in Catherine's words about change "OK, that's not working, move on. Let's just change it up."

Proposition 2: *Collegial, Professional Relationships Provide Instructional Support to Beginning Teachers.*
Participating in peer observations and a learning community helped the beginning teachers to connect to each other and to the faculty they observed, thereby building relationships that offered support that helped the beginning teachers grow professionally. Trust in the community was foundational to the learning community setting. Participants showed their comfort level with the group by taking risks and making themselves vulnerable. They revealed their

fears and concerns by using language such as "I am battling with," "I am struggling with," "My biggest concern right now is," and "I have a student in my classroom and I don't know how to motivate him."

The participants shared concerns, asked questions, shared successes, and sought solutions during these learning community sessions. Their willingness to make themselves vulnerable may stem from their view of the learning community. Many participants spoke of the learning community as a place of commonality—a level playing field.

The beginning teachers were much more candid in the learning community setting than with their teams during their weekly team meetings. Many participants addressed this difference. Team meetings were viewed by most as a time for talking through curriculum issues. Catherine voiced the role of team meetings as "what we are going to teach, how we are going to teach it, and big ideas about content and teaching."

According to Ginny, in learning communities, "We talk more about our challenges and how some of us had similar challenges and we try to give strategies to help fix those ... challenges." The beginning teachers felt that both meetings supported them in their work. They just had different purposes. The team meeting is more focused on using the veteran teachers' expertise to plan and pace instruction, and the learning community is focused on solving problems.

Catherine mentioned that peer observation had "opened up a line of communication" between herself and the peers that she had observed. Going into someone's classroom to observe implies communication. Typically, the beginning teacher and the teacher he or she is to observe have a conversation before and after the observation. Teachers are building connections through professional conversations about practice. Teachers that do not work at the same grade level or on the same hall are talking about instruction.

This level of support has lowered the emotional threat level in the building. It is okay for a peer to ask you questions about how you do things or come and watch you work, and it is flattering to be asked. As Ginny said, "I didn't really think anything [I was doing in my classroom] would really help anyone else."

Participating in peer observations and in a learning community has given beginning teachers numerous opportunities to see and hear what teaching and learning are like in their school. These opportunities to engage in observation and conversation work to negate isolation, give participants a more accurate perspective of their work, and provide a context for instruction within the school.

Ginny stated that participating in peer observations and learning community "let me know that I'm on the right track and that ... for the most part we are going in the same direction." Several participants mentioned that their experiences in the study gave their confidence a boost. Ginny captured this by saying, "Hey, I am OK ... they're doing the same thing, you know?"

Proposition 3: *Beginning Teachers Can Embrace Reflective Practice.*
The beginning teachers that participated in this study spoke extensively about the thinking that they do about teaching. Denise feels that the way to "use what you have seen is through reflection." Edward shared that reflection "allows [him] to take ... information and digest it." Through reflection, he has figured out that "in order to be a teacher, you have to be a learner." Figuring out how what you have seen or heard applies to you, implies change, and according to Denise, "you have the freedom to do that [change]."

Beginning teachers are thinking, articulating concerns, observing others, and shifting their practice based on the data they collect from other teachers. This type of reflective practice levels the playing field between veterans and beginning teachers by accelerating the competency process. Edward believes that teaching is a job that you get better at as you gain experience. He stated, "By observing others ... you get more experience." Beth said peer observations have "helped me get up to speed ... reach competency quicker. I probably didn't have to fail as many times because I had the opportunity to see someone else."

The reflective thinking helped the beginning teachers shift their focus off themselves and onto students, making their teaching more responsive to students' needs. Catherine and Beth both spoke to the idea that their concerns had shifted over the course of the first semester. When school began, they were concerned about where to put stuff and how to get through the day. Beth admitted, "I never thought about multiple teaching strategies at the beginning of the year."

By the close of the first semester, however, the focus had shifted to students. Beth illustrated that shift when she said, "I want to know multiple ways of doing things so that I can give them [the students] different strategies and different ways to look at it." In addition, Edward feels that he is learning different "techniques and styles that will enhance my teaching experience which will help students get it sooner."

During an interview, Catherine explained that when she goes on a peer observation, she not only watches the teacher but she is also now watching the students. Catherine commented: "When you are not having to be the one worried about the teaching ... you're watching the kids who are just like the kids in your classroom. Who are ... not engaged in it at all, or don't get it, or are just kind of lost. And, when you go back in your class, then you kind of remember that." Comments like these represent the shift in thinking from self to student that occurred during this study.

The change to a focus on students has also shifted the talk in learning community sessions to topics like differentiation and multiple teaching strategies. Edward has figured out "there is no set way to teach and trying to teach one paramount way over another … sets you up for failure." Adam believes that his "bag of tools" has increased because of his involvement with peer observation and learning community. Learning for Adam centers on the idea "that it is going to take more than one strategy for anything."

The reflective practice that was focused on meeting the instructional needs of students represents a mature understanding of the nature of teaching. Finding ways to engage all students and bring the curriculum to the student means that you can set aside your own needs and focus on the needs of others. Ginny expressed it this way: "It makes sense … if you have a student and you give him all of that support … and you give him other resources … then naturally he's going to succeed." Success is a great motivating force for students and teachers.

## DISCUSSION OF FINDINGS

This study built on research about beginning teachers, peer observation, and learning communities. Patterns emerged which then formed the foundation for the themes.

Theme 1: *Peer observation and learning communities are strong instructional supports for beginning teachers, but they may not be enough by themselves to support fully beginning teachers.*
Support structures for beginning teachers must be multidimensional, well-articulated, and focused. Beginning teachers need time to work one on one with a veteran, time with other beginning teachers, and time with veteran teachers. At the research site, beginning teachers had a mentor that worked one on one with them in a well-articulated, structured relationship. The participants had the opportunity to participate in peer observations and a learning community of beginning teachers.

Both these experiences were structured and clearly communicated. In addition, all teachers met weekly with their teams during the day to plan instruction and talk through matters of curriculum and twice monthly after school with the extended team to collaborate and communicate. Furthermore, teams met monthly for Team Learning Community for a two-hour period with the instructional coach to plan instruction on a larger scale and to further their learning.

**Theme 2:** *Peer observations and learning community are strong instructional supports when the culture and climate of the school honors practitioner research that is teacher directed.*

Denise mentioned that in some schools, the peer-observation experience would not be successful because going to watch a peer was an admission of failure. The principal at the research site modeled a leadership style that valued teachers and honored teacher learning. The principal encouraged teachers to think and to try new things, respected teachers as professionals, cared about her staff both professionally and personally, and held high expectations for teachers.

Because she had been the principal of this school for ten years, she has had time to build leadership within her staff that "lives" her values. Additionally, she has also tuned into staff morale and has worked to keep morale high. This principal is comfortable with empowering teachers to make choices that guide their own professional learning. Working in a school for a leader that trusts and respects teachers and their work makes taking professional risks palatable for the teaching staff.

**Theme 3:** *Peer observations and learning communities are strong instructional supports when the right amount and type of accountability is present.*

Each month the learning community met so that the members could share their questions of practice, what they learned from their peer observations, and what their next steps were. This accountability piece put the right amount of gentle pressure on participants to follow through with their observations without making the process feel mandated or pushed down. Care was taken to mandate little other than the expectation that each participant would observe a peer each month, work within the action research model, and attend learning community meetings.

No mandated forms or charts were used to observe peers, and participants were not questioned about whether they had done their observation that month. No one accompanied participants to their observations either. Instead, the learning community acted as a palatable accountability piece for the community of beginning teachers by applying positive peer pressure on the group to live up to the expectations presented.

**Theme 4:** *Peer observations and learning communities provide avenues for teachers to learn about themselves professionally.*

All participants spoke about the perspective they had gained by participating in peer observations and learning community. That perspective was multifaceted. First, participants realized that they were doing a good job in their own classrooms. Beth and Ginny both said in their interviews that after observing their first peer, they realized they were doing similar things in their own classrooms so they must be OK. Second, several participants mentioned that observing across the building gave them a better perspective about what teaching looked like across the grade levels in the school.

Catherine mentioned that this vertical look gave her a better idea of where she fits into the big picture of teaching at the school. Several participants mentioned that observing building-wide opened and encouraged communication across the entire faculty. Finally, observing other teachers gave participants opportunities to observe other teacher's students. Beth and Catherine believed that this helped them better understand their own students.

Beth talked about being more confident to gauge expectations for her students because of peer observation. Catherine mentioned that watching other teachers work with unmotivated or misbehaving students gave her ideas about how to handle those same types of students in her own classroom. Ginny said that watching other teachers handle disengaged students affirmed her own practice because those teachers use the same types of strategies that she uses.

Theme 5: *Peer observations and learning communities help participants develop new ideas about teaching and learning.*
The participants talked about the value of gaining multiple strategies to teach students because through this process of peer observation and meeting in a learning community they all began to understand that it is their job to bring the learning to the student. Many of the participants talked about differentiating the curriculum for a student or devising behavior plans to help a student. Denise talked about her new understanding related to the idea that you must teach students things "over and over again." "One big lesson won't do."

In addition, the participants reported content-driven learning as well. Denise tightened up the structure she used in her reading groups. Beth and Catherine learned how to run literacy centers while teaching guided reading. Edward observed mathematics classes in the grades leading up to his to understand how to approach mathematical learning in his grade level. Adam learned to use Touch Math with the new student that came in that was so far behind, whereas Ginny learned songs that teach content from her observations. As Adam said, "You can always learn something from somebody."

How peer observations and learning communities affect students is unclear because data are anecdotal; however, all participants felt strongly that students were positively affected. Ginny spoke about watching her students implement strategies while doing independent work that she taught them that came from a peer observation. Adam mentioned that his students' writing had gotten a lot better because he now knew to do some things differently.

Because of her experience with peer observation and learning community, Denise felt that she was holding her students to a higher accountability level for their own learning, and they were meeting that expectation. Beth and Catherine felt that just watching their students during centers was evidence that peer observations and learning community had positively impacted their students. As Catherine explained, "Everything I know to do I got from my peer observations."

Finally, several of the participants talked about how the opportunity to observe their peers gave them some teaching strategies that worked to try with their own students. In other words, they did not have to fail as much by figuring this out on their own through trial and error. Perhaps students were positively affected by this lessening of failure on the teacher's part. Maybe students did as well as they did because their teacher brought tested strategies in the classroom instead of untested strategies.

## IMPLICATIONS FOR SCHOOL LEADERS

To suggest that beginning teachers need instructional support is not new; however, this study sought to learn about supporting beginning teachers by giving them an opportunity to participate in a peer-observation experience and in a learning community. Based on the findings from this research, the following implications for school leaders are offered.

### Begin Peer Observations in Your School

Peer observations and learning communities provide instructional support for beginning teachers; however, few teachers ever participate in a peer observation. At the minimum, begin the process of peer observation in small nonthreatening ways in your school for the entire staff. Involving teacher leaders in this process will bring cooperation to this new experience. Scheduling the observations and providing time to debrief about them will bring accountability to the process, ensuring that peer observations happen and reflection follows.

If question posing is foreign to the staff, it might be appropriate to frame the observation with a guiding question that is the same for everyone. Perhaps this question should reflect building instructional priorities that are tightly focused and observable. For example, a guiding question could focus on what student engagement looks like in that classroom or on teacher questioning.

## Ensure That the Professional Development in Your School Is Multidimensional

Peer observations and learning communities provide optimal instructional support for beginning teachers when they are a part of a multilayered approach to job-embedded professional learning. Step back and look at the professional-development opportunities that your district and school offers. Here are some questions to ponder:

- Is the purpose of each piece clear and well-articulated?
- Are there opportunities for teams to plan collaboratively?
- Is leadership being built within the teaching corps?
- Do beginning teachers have opportunities to work with a mentor to improve instruction?
- Do beginning teachers have opportunities to work with other beginning teachers?

When professional learning is viewed as multilayered with each layer serving a distinct purpose and focused on change, the learning of the entire faculty is enhanced.

### Examine the Culture and Climate of Your School

Culture and climate in the work environment impact teaching and learning. Examine your leadership practices noting those that promote trust, respect, communication, and build relationships and those practices that do not. How can you strengthen the culture and climate of your school by intentionally enhancing some of your practices and discarding others? What kind of professional learning do you need to improve the culture and climate of your school to one that will support a structured peer observation and learning community process?

### Work with Someone to Implement Multilayered Professional Development in Your School

Finally, if possible, work with an instructional coach, a professional-development coordinator, and teacher–leaders to implement a multilayered professional-development plan that includes peer observations and learning community sessions for beginning teachers. Dispatch the instructional coach to build relationships and rapport with these beginning teachers as individuals and to work to bring the group together as a community of learners. The momentum for this work was maintained by incorporating peer observation and learning communities into the daily work of the school.

## SUMMARY

This intersection of peer observation and collaboration refines planning and interpersonal skills and improves teaching practices. The implementation of a peer observation process that allows beginning teachers to meet in learning community supports the findings related to collaboration and peer observation. In this study, teachers were allowed to direct their learning, reflect on their learning, and collaborate with others, which caused shifts in teaching to take place that reflected layers of understanding. Catherine spoke to this when she said, "Peer observation put me in charge of my learning. It [peer observation] has opened up a line of communication with peers."

Continual professional development through a learning community is a powerful way to integrate beginning teachers into the work of the school and to give them guidance for their daily work. The beginning teachers that participated in this study spoke to the powerful experience that learning communities were to them. In addition, the participants credited their work in peer observations and learning community with negating the isolation that new teachers typically feel.

### Discussion Questions

1. Do peer observations and learning community fit with the other pieces of professional learning in your building? What are your next steps to ensure that the professional learning in your building is multilayered and clearly articulated?
2. Think about the culture and climate of your school. What kind of shifts need to be made before you introduce peer observations and learning community to your school?
3. What are the barriers to implementing peer observations and learning community? How will you remove those barriers?

## SUGGESTED READINGS

Clement, M. C. (2016). *Retaining effective teachers: A guide for hiring, induction, and support*. Lanham, MD: Rowman & Littlefield.
Kise, J. A. G. (2017). *Differentiated coaching: A framework for helping educators change* (2nd ed.). Thousand Oaks, CA: Corwin Press.

Zepeda, S. J. (2015). *Job-embedded professional development: Support, collaboration, and learning in schools.* New York: Routledge.

## REFERENCES

Bickmore, D. L., & Bickmore, S. T. (2010). A multifaceted approach to teacher induction. *Teaching and Teacher Education*, 26(4), 1006–1014. doi: 10.1016/j. tate.2009.10.043

DeNeve, D., & Devos, G. (2017). How do professional learning communities aid and hamper professional learning of beginning teachers related to differentiated instruction? *Teachers and Teaching Theory and Practice*, 23(3), 262–283. doi: http:// dx.doi.org/10.1080/13540602.2016.1206524

DeAngelis, K. J., & Presley, J. B. (2011). Toward a more nuanced understanding of new teacher attrition. *Education and Urban Society*, 43(5), 598–626. doi: 10.1177/0013124510380724

DuFour, R., & Eaker, R. (1998). *Professional learning communities at work: Best practices for enhancing student achievement.* Bloomington, IN: Solution Tree.

Fiszer, E. (2004). *How teachers learn best: An ongoing professional development model.* Lanham, MD: Scarecrow Education.

Gilbert, L. (2005). What helps beginning teachers? *Educational Leadership*, 62(8), 36. Retrieved from http://www.ascd.org/publications/educational-leadership.aspx

Glaser, B., & Strauss, A. (1967). *The discovery of grounded theory: Strategies for qualitative research.* Chicago: Aldine.

Glickman, C. D., Gordon, S. P., & Ross-Gordon, J. M. (2017). *SuperVision and instructional leadership: A developmental approach* (10th ed.). Boston: Pearson.

Goldring, R., Taie, S., & Riddles, M. (2014). Teacher attrition and mobility: Results from the 2012–13 Teacher Follow-up Survey (NCES 2014-077). US Department of Education. Washington, DC: National Center for Education Statistics. Retrieved from http://nces.ed.gov/pubs2014/2014077.pdf

Gordon, S. P. (2016). Framing instructional supervision. In J. Glanz & S. J. Zepeda, *Supervision: New perspectives for theory and practice* (pp. 23–41). Lanham, MD: Rowman & Littlefield.

Grossman, P., Wineburg, S., & Woolworth, S. (2000). What makes teacher community different from a gathering of teachers? An occasional paper. Albany, NY: National Research Center on English Learning and Achievement and the University of Washington: Center for the Study of Teaching and Policy.

Guskey, T. (2000). *Evaluating professional development.* Thousand Oaks, CA: Corwin Press.

Hammersley-Fletcher, L., & Orsmond, P. (2004). Evaluating our peers: Is peer observation a meaningful process? *Studies in Higher Education*, 29(4), 489–503. doi: http://dx.doi.org/10.1080/0307507042000236380

Harris, A., & Jones, M. (2010). Professional learning communities and system improvement. *Improving Schools*, 13(2), 172–181. doi: 10.1177/1365480210376487

He, Y., & Cooper, J. (2011). Struggles and strategies in teaching: Voices of five novice secondary teachers. *Teacher Education Quarterly*, 38(2), 97–116. Retrieved from http://www.jstor.org/stable/23479695

Ingersoll, R. M. (2012). Beginning teacher induction: What the data tell us. *Phi Delta Kappan,* 93(8), 47–51. doi: 10.1177/003172171209300811

Ingersoll, R. M., & Strong M. (2011). The impact of induction and mentoring programs for beginning teachers: A critical review of the research. *Review of Educational Research*, 81(2), 201–233. doi: 10.3102/0034654311403323

Joftus, S., & Maddox-Dolan, B. (2002). *New-teacher excellence: Retaining our best.* Washington, DC: Alliance for Excellent Education.

Johnson, S., Berg, J., & Donaldson, M. (2005). *Who stays in teaching and why: A review of the literature on teacher retention.* Cambridge, MA: Harvard University.

Joyce, B., & Showers, B. (1995). *Student achievement through staff development* (2nd ed.). White Plains, NY: Longman.

Kardos, S. M., & Johnson, S. M. (2010). New teachers' experiences of mentoring: The good, the bad, and the inequity. *Journal of Educational Change*, 11(1), 23–44. doi:10.1007/s10833-008-9096-3

Katzenmeyer, M., & Moller, G. (2009). *Awakening the sleeping giant: Helping teachers develop as leaders* (3rd ed.). Thousand Oaks, CA: Corwin Press.

Meanwell, E., & Kleiner, S. (2014). The emotional experience of first-time teaching: Reflections from graduate instructors, 1997–2006. *Teaching Sociology*, 42(1), 17–27. doi: 10.1177/0092055X13508377

Mee, M., & Haverback, H.R. (2014). Commitment, preparation, and early career frustrations: Examining future attrition of middle school teachers. *American Secondary Education*, 42(3), 39–51. Retrieved from https://www.ashland.edu/coe/about-college/american-secondary-education-journal

Merriam, S. B., & Tisdell, E. J. (2015). *Qualitative research: A guide to design and implementation* (4th ed.). San Francisco: Jossey-Bass.

Miranda, T. T. (2012). Lessons learned from transformational professional development. (pp. 77–88). In M. Golden (Ed.), *Teaching and learning from the inside out: Revitalizing ourselves and our institutions*. New Direction for Teaching and Learning, Number 130, Summer. San Francisco: Jossey-Bass.

National Commission on Teaching and America's Future. (2003). Unraveling the teacher shortage problem: Teacher retention is key. Washington, DC: National Commission on Teaching and America's Future. Author.

National Commission on Teaching and America's Future. (2005). *No dream denied: A pledge to America's children*. Washington, DC: National Commission on Teaching and America's Future. Author.

Parker, M. A., Ndoye, A., & Imig, S. R. (2009). Keeping our teachers! Investigating mentoring practices to support and retain novice educators. *Mentoring & Tutoring: Partnership in Learning*, 17(4), 329–341. doi: 10.1080/13611260903391500

Ragin, C., & Becker, H. (Eds.). (1992). *What is a case? Exploring the foundations of social inquiry.* New York: Cambridge University Press.

Veenman, S. (1984). Perceived problems of beginning teachers. *Review of Educational Research*, 54(2), 143–178. Retrieved from http://journals.sagepub.com/toc/rera/54/2

Wong, H. (2002). Induction: The best form of professional development. *Educational Leadership*, 59(6), 52–54. Retrieved from http://www.ascd.org/publications/educational-leadership.aspx

Zepeda, S. J. (2012). *Professional development: What works* (2nd ed.). New York: Routledge.

Zepeda, S. J. (2015). *Job-embedded professional development: Support, collaboration, and learning in schools*. New York: Routledge.

Zepeda, S. J. (2017). *Instructional supervision: Applying tools and concepts* (4th ed.). New York: Routledge.

5

# Lessons about Job-Embedded Coaching

Sally J. Zepeda

Key Ideas in This Chapter …

- Sense of belonging
- Support from colleagues
- Lessons for School Leaders
- Final thoughts

Throughout each chapter, numerous lessons about the nature of coaching as a form of job-embedded professional learning are identified. The authors identify and discuss the types of supports that school leaders need to ensure are available for teachers to grow and to develop. Through the case studies, the authors have illuminated how coaching can be enacted and the structures that support the development of coaching for teachers and the instructional coaches who work with them.

This chapter examines sense of belonging, social learning theories, key supports associated with coaching, and then concludes with lessons for school leaders to consider related to their work with teachers.

## SENSE OF BELONGING

Feeling and experiencing a sense of belonging is important for all teachers, most especially new teachers during the first years of teaching. Beginning teachers have recently concluded their clinical experiences including student teaching and now are on their own. The issues first-year teachers experience can be daunting as described in chapter 1. Isolation, the need for leader and peer support, and other issues including dealing with the complexities of

79

the curriculum and instruction for students who come to the classroom with various needs make a persuasive case for the need for coaching.

The sense of belonging that teachers experience is examined through Maslow's (1943) hierarchy of needs. Figure 5.1 illustrates that at the bottom of the pyramid are basic needs such as food, water, warmth, and rest. Immediately above these are safety needs including security. These two layers of the hierarchy are basic needs.

The next two layers are psychological needs—belongingness and esteem needs. Belongingness is a general sense that one belongs and has relationships with others. Positioned in the middle of the hierarchy, a sense of belonging, or belongingness, is the need to feel connected to other people and to engage in relationships (Rogers, 1951). Baumeister and Leary (1995) suggest that "human beings have a pervasive drive to form and maintain at least a minimum quantity of lasting, positive, and significant interpersonal relationships" (p. 497).

According to Kelly (2001), those who do not have their sense of belonging needs met can experience isolation very much like teachers who often work independently in their classrooms. A sense of belonging is important for teachers to be able to:

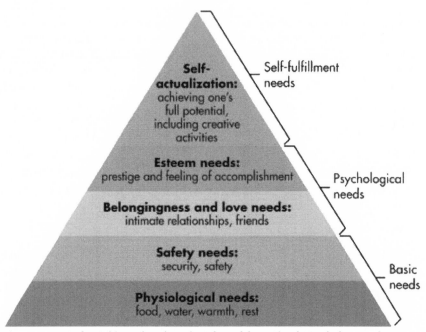

Figure 5.1   Maslow's hierarchy of needs. Adapted from SimplyPsychology (n.d.)

- Experience meaning from their work;
- Increase commitment to the profession;
- Feel part of the school and its community—teachers, students, administrators, families;
- Grow and learn from their work;
- Feel valued; and
- Continue to be motivated during stressful aspects of teaching and working with students (Allen, 2009; Dranitsaris, n.d.; Huppert, 2017)

Beginning teachers need to sense that they belong as they receive support from their colleagues who coach them through the beginning stages of their careers. Teachers across the career continuum share, albeit at diverse levels, the same need to belong and to work with supportive colleagues.

## SUPPORT FROM COLLEAGUES

Historically, teachers—most devastatingly beginning teachers—typically work in isolation with limited interactions with their peers (Lortie, 1975; Zepeda & Ponticell, 1997). However, in recent years, schools have been encouraged to establish an "integrated professional culture" where schools (1) promote consistent interaction among teachers across experience levels, (2) recognize and validate novices' needs as beginners, and (3) develop shared responsibility among teachers for the school and its students (Kardos & Johnson, 2007; Kardos, Johnson, Peske, Kauffman, & Liu, 2001).

This collective approach positions beginning teachers as active participants in their own learning and in becoming contributing members of their school communities by focusing on collaboration as the key ingredient to success. Beginning teachers want and need to collaborate in their first years of teaching. They need coaches and "experienced colleagues who will take their daily dilemmas seriously, watch them teach and provide feedback, help them develop instructional strategies, model skilled teaching, and share insights about students' work and lives" (Johnson & Kardos, 2002, p. 13).

### Collaboration

Beginning teachers see collaboration as an opportunity to share, learn, and grow while building quality relationships with their peers. Research on collaboration illustrates that it has positive effects on student achievement, school culture, and professional learning (Bryk, Sebring, Allensworth, Luppescu, & Easton, 2010; Glazerman et al., 2010). Moreover, collaboration and trust are foundational for job-embedded professional development to flourish.

Collaboration allows for an exchange of ideas through purposeful conversations, provides opportunities for teachers to support their own learning as well as the learning of their colleagues, focuses efforts on the overall enhancement of instructional skills, and leads to higher levels of student achievement (Goddard & Goddard, 2007; Louis, Marks, & Kruse, 1996; Newmann & Wehlage, 1995).

By providing beginning teachers with opportunities to collaborate with colleagues they are in a better position to co-construct knowledge about teaching and learning. In collaborative cultures, professional development becomes communal and job-embedded (Cole, 2018). Darling-Hammond, Wei, Andree, Richardson, and Orphanos (2009) advocated, "[c]ollaborative approaches to professional learning can promote school change that extends beyond individual classrooms—when all teachers in a school learn together, all students in the school benefit" (p. 5).

Collaborative time between beginning teachers and their colleagues allows them to

- share information,
- get advice,
- construct and reconstruct understandings of policy,
- learn about acceptable instructional approaches,
- gain time management skills, and
- navigate relationships with students and parents. (Kardos et al., 2001; Qian, Youngs, & Frank, 2013)

Collaboration is important in that "teachers want to belong; they want to have peers to turn to for support. Schools with collaborative cultures build camaraderie and send a strong, positive message about the serious nature of teaching" (Zepeda, 2015, p. 5).

## Social Learning Theory

Social learning theory (Bandura, 1977) stresses the importance of observing and modeling behaviors, supporting communication patterns, and learning from the emotional behaviors and the reactions of others. Bandura explained the interrelated nature of observing and modeling behaviors in this way, "fortunately, most human behavior is learned observationally through modeling: from observing others form an idea of how new behaviors are performed, and on later occasions this coded information serves as a guide for action" (p. 22).

Translating the interrelated nature of observing and modeling, coaching provides processes and a context to support social learning with its emphasis on interactions, conversations, coaching cycles that include classroom observations, and modeling during team meetings, professional learning sessions, etc. In a coaching relationship, both the coach and the teacher being coached are active learners; this is called *reciprocal learning.*

A coach can support social learning with teachers by attending to four processes associated with modeling, a key aspect of work that coaches engage in as they work with teachers. The four processes with descriptions and coaching applications are offered in Table 5.1.

## Pushing the Boundaries in the Zone of Proximal Development

Aligned with Bandura, Vygotsky (1978) believed that people do not learn in isolation, that learning is a social endeavor, and that knowledge is socially constructed through interactions with others. Coaching is a highly social and interactive process that supports teachers in the further development of knowledge, application of skills, and refinement of practices.

Coaches work with teachers who come to the school house with varying levels of experience, content knowledge, familiarity with students, and myriad variables that affect student learning. Coaches work with teachers "where they are," inching them toward improved classroom instruction and routines. Vygotsky's theory, the Zone of Proximal Development (ZPD), is apt for coaches to consider.

The ZPD is a place where a teacher's skill level presently exists. Through coaching, teachers are led through learning with the coach and teacher both working toward improving practice levels up from the starting point. Akin to the 5K runner, the coach is on the sidelines encouraging and motivating teachers to push through, slowing down slightly after the finish line, running in place, but not stopping.

Learning in the ZPD is socially constructed with the coach engaging in processes to promote growth. These processes would include, for example, conversations leading to inquiry and reflection on practice. For beginning teachers, this type of support and guidance in improving instruction is important given the high attrition within the first five years in the profession (see discussion in chapter 1). Moreover, the beliefs, attitudes, and foundational practices learned during the first years of teaching more than likely follow that teacher through the career.

Coaches can go a long way in modeling that learning to teach is a lifetime endeavor and that learning to teach is an ongoing process. Coaches help build a learning community where the focus is on adults learning to become more effective in the classroom. The more teachers learn, the more students learn.

School leaders support coaching as a job-embedded form of professional learning. Chapter authors Lakesha Robinson Goff, Angela K. Rainwater,

**Table 5.1  Four Processes Associated with Modeling**

| Process | Description | Coaching Applications and Beliefs |
|---------|-------------|------------------------------------|
| *Attention* | For behaviors to be successfully learned, the individual must pay sufficient attention. | Coaches<br>-engage teachers as active participants in the coaching process;<br>-use strategies that are mindful of the adult learner (relevance, immediate application, etc.). |
| *Retention* | Storing this information so that it may be used at a later date is crucial to the observational learning process. | Coaches<br>-focus on content-based materials to engage teachers in job-embedded activities;<br>-visit classrooms to observe teacher transfer of content to the classroom. |
| *Reproduction* | Following attention and retention comes the time to reproduce the observed behavior. Practice of this behavior assists with the improvement of skills. | Coaches<br>-engage in modeling, co-teaching, and other arrangements that promote applying what is learned, professionally, in classrooms;<br>-engage in conversations about what was observed, develop action plans to extend learning in follow-up learning opportunities. |
| *Motivation* | The individual must be motivated to repeat the learned behavior. Reinforcement and punishment influence assist to influence this step as it acts to either encourage or deter the individual from having the motivation to repeat the modeled behavior. | Coaches<br>-motivate through affirming the efforts of teaching, even when mid-course modifications need to be collaboratively developed to support improvement;<br>-hold accountability but do *not* punish teachers with punitive consequences;<br>-build relationships with teachers and gain trust with teachers. |

Adapted from Learning Theories. (n.d.); Vicarious Reinforcement and Imitative Learning. (n.d.).

and Susan Hare Bolen amplify the findings of their case studies with the implications and lessons for school leaders to consider.

## LESSONS FOR SCHOOL LEADERS

By reviewing the three case studies, several lessons can be drawn from the findings. The lessons are offered to give school leaders ideas to reflect on about job-embedded learning and coaching—regardless of form. A caveat is offered: school leaders and teachers need to examine these lessons as points of departure because job-embedded learning and coaching must be contextualized within the individual school. The conceptualizations will be influenced by the history of past efforts, the characteristics of teachers and their experiences with professional learning and coaching, and so many more variables that make a school as unique as the teachers in the building.

To assist school personnel in thinking about the contextual variables that need to be examined to frame beliefs, a few ideas about job-embedded coaching are presented in Table 5.2. Long-term planning is needed to ensure that beliefs and practices are in alignment. Without such alignment, coherence is not likely.

### Thinking about Job-Embedded Learning

As a review, job-embedded learning is highly-contextualized and personalized based on the developmental and differentiated needs of teachers (Zepeda, 2015). There are five overall foundations of job-embedded learning:

- Holds relevance for the adult learner—Adults want to be successful and derive value from their learning. Job-embedded learning is highly individualized.
- Includes feedback as part of the process—Job-embedded learning includes feedback and collaborative supports as a built-in process (e.g., peer coaching).
- Supports inquiry and reflection—Job-embedded learning promotes thinking more critically and reflectively about practice. This reflection can be done at the individual level or as a group.
- Facilitates the transfer of new skills into practice—Job-embedded learning provides ongoing support, which is linked to transferring learned skills into practice.
- Promotes collaboration—It is through collaboration that teachers share with one another, engage in discussions, and reflect about their experiences. (Zepeda, 2015, pp. 35–38).

**Table 5.2 Examining Contextual Variables**

| | |
|---|---|
| Context of the school | -Type of school (urban, suburban, rural, high school, elementary, middle, public, private, parochial, military, etc.);<br>-School demographics (size, number of students, number of teachers, composition of the administrative team);<br>-Other areas that make the school context unique (e.g., theme school, charter school, block schedule, teacher attrition rates, socioeconomic status), etc. |
| Teacher characteristics | -Number of teachers in the building;<br>-Number of years in teaching (beginning teacher, etc.);<br>-Number of years at present school setting;<br>-Highest degree held, etc.;<br>-Type of preparation (e.g., traditional, alternative); and<br>-Highly qualified (certification status). |
| Structure of the day for professional learning | Professional learning occurs primarily:<br>-During planning<br>-Before school<br>-After school<br>-Professional learning days<br>-Preplanning days<br>-Postplanning days<br>Daily Schedule<br>-Do teachers have individual and group planning time (e.g., grade level, content area, etc.);<br>-Weekly scheduled time;<br>-Use of faculty meetings, digital platforms, etc. available for professional learning. |
| Administrator expertise and support | -Types of ongoing support that can be provided for teachers and by whom;<br>-How efforts are monitored;<br>-Do teachers and leaders learn alongside one another? |
| Teacher involvement | -How are teachers involved in planning, ongoing assessment, and evaluation of professional learning?<br>-Have teachers assumed leadership roles (e.g., peer coach, book study leader?)?<br>-Are teachers decision makers about their professional learning?<br>-Do teachers take the lead in delivering professional learning? |

Adapted from Zepeda (2017). Course Syllabus for Learning Communities and Staff Development. University of Georgia.

**Table 5.3. Key Aspects and Features of Job-Embedded Learning**

Embedded within the workday and relevant to teacher needs

Extended over time, allowing teachers enough time to interact with colleagues (e.g., coaching, modeling, etc.)

Continuous, ongoing, with planned follow-up

Coherent with state standards, school policies, and practices

Content- and grade-specific to teachers' subject matter

Designed according to the principles of adult learning

Promotes collaboration, brainstorming, reflection, and inquiry

Uses student data to frame and assess learning needs

Evaluated and assessed on an ongoing basis

Adapted from Croft, Coggshall, Dolan, Powers, & Killion, 2010; Darling-Hammond, Hyler, & Gardner; 2017; Desimone, 2009, 2011; Desimone & Garet, 2015; Guskey, 2014; Zepeda, 2015.

The research on job-embedded learning illustrates key aspects of effective and useful programs and features (Darling-Hammond, Hyler, & Gardner, 2017; Desimone, 2009; Desimone & Garet, 2015). The key aspects and features of job-embedded learning are illustrated in Table 5.3.

The needs of teachers at the beginning of their careers are different than the needs of teachers who are at the mid-point or the end of their careers. Regardless of experience, level of education, and so on, all teachers have learning needs that can be met from examining their practices with the support of a coach. The expression, *everyone needs a coach*, is especially critical given the complexities of teaching and the students who populate classrooms.

There is a nexus between student and teacher as active learners that Calvert (2016) aptly captures: "If we want our students to engage in rich, creative learning experiences that lead to mastery, then we must provide educators with rich, creative learning experiences that lead to mastery" (p. 10). This thought applies to teachers throughout their careers.

## Lessons Learned

Numerous lessons for school leaders emerged from the works of the authors. As a reminder, each chapter ends with a section titled, *Implications for School Leaders*. The implications within each chapter are based logically on the findings of the study. Embedded within these implications are suggestions for school leaders to consider as they lead job-embedded coaching and professional learning. The lessons drawn from the three cases provide opportunity for school leaders to think about coaching as a viable option to support job-embedded learning. The following lessons are examined.

### Lesson 1: Job-Embedded Coaching Affirms Teachers as Adult Learners

Adults seek many ways to learn. Adults are self-directed learners that find motivation to participate in learning experiences that focus on tasks that relate to their daily lives (Knowles, 1973). Knowles (1973) and Knowles, Holton, and Swanson (2011) identified key principles of adult learning that influence the ways in which adults learn and the conditions in which they learn.

- Adults are internally motivated and self-directed.
- Adults bring life experiences and knowledge to learning experiences.
- Adults are goal oriented.
- Adults are relevancy oriented.
- Adults are practical.
- Adult learners like to be respected; they require a collaborative, respectful, mutual, and an informal climate.

In chapter 4, Bolen presents descriptions and findings about a specialized learning community that was established for first-year teachers. In this learning community, teachers were able to interact with one another formally every month. In between learning community meetings, the first-year teachers observed veteran teachers in their classrooms, and they engaged in conversations.

There are two overall messages in this case study. First, the new teachers were learning how to ask for help and assistance. Second, these first-year teachers were being socialized into the profession in a culture that embraces supporting teachers and one in which all teachers are learners.

The structure of the monthly learning community meetings was open-ended to allow the first-year teachers to identify what was most pressing to explore and to engage in discussions in a safe space. These first-year teachers were the decision makers; they had agency over their explorations. Agency is important for job-embedded forms of professional learning, including coaching, to evolve in schools. Calvert (2016) shares that teacher agency is *"The capacity of teachers to act purposefully and constructively to direct their professional growth and contribute to the growth of their colleagues"* (p. 4, emphasis in the original).

The topical areas examined during meetings were generated from what was occurring in their classrooms and the lingering questions from classroom observations. Bills, Giles, and Rogers (2016) offer the perspective that

We know that beginning teachers need to have a professional knowledge of teaching (knowing) and professional practices in teaching (doing). They are at their best in the classroom when they are supported by their colleagues in appreciatively supportive ways to know how best to improve and integrate their practice. (p. 118)

Throughout this self-directed learning process, Bolen reminds us that the first-year teachers were given both the flexibility and the opportunity to reflect on their learning while working together with their peers in a collegial setting.

In chapter 2, Goff examines coaching conversations from the perspectives of five first-year teachers in a large urban setting. Goff found that time and space in daily school life for novice teachers and their coaches is requisite for fruitful coaching conversations that served to meet the needs of teachers. Through the coaching conversations, the teachers were able to ask for advice, follow-up with "burning questions," and otherwise receive support needed that best fit the context of their situations.

As a support structure, Goff's findings illustrate that for first-year teachers, coaching conversations that are "productive" include opportunities for them to envision their future, to be affirmed, to learn from the expertise of the coach, and to engage in inquiry to build skills and confidence.

The findings from both Bolen and Goff's chapters are important as Bills et al. (2016) remind us, "[n]ew teachers cannot be expected to 'see' and 'notice' every aspect of the complexities of being a good teacher in the classroom without the support of more experienced colleagues" (p. 116).

## Lesson 2: Job-Embedded Coaching Affirms the Teacher as a Decision Maker

In chapter 4, Bolen examined a special learning community established for beginning teachers. In the structure provided by the school's instructional coach, teachers met monthly as a group, and they engaged in various activities outside of the monthly learning community meetings. They observed more veteran teachers in their classrooms and engaged in conversations after the classroom observations.

During monthly learning community meetings, the teachers were empowered to shape what occurred. The content of the monthly meetings was directed by the teachers and based on self-identified learning needs including what they were experiencing in their own classrooms, topical interests based on the students they taught, and the lessons they were learning through observing teachers.

Did any of these teachers struggle? Of course, they did. They were in their first years of teaching; however, the teachers were in an environment that supported taking risks, learning about their teaching practices, and exercising agency about what was most important to focus on. The lesson learned from this study is that even teachers who struggle can make decisions about what's most important and why, and moreover, if empowered, they can take action on what's needed.

### Lesson 3: Job-Embedded Coaching Includes Support Structures

Across the chapters, the authors describe and explain the various support structures involved in job-embedded learning for adults. For Goff (chapter 2), targeted conversations during coaching opportunities assisted teacher learning. The power and potential behind every coaching conversation emerged as a key lever of effective practice. Coaching conversations are not casual dialogues where the coach holds all the power. Instead, they are organic discussions in which the novice's voice is appreciated and respected. Although coaches and novices engage in several activities including co-planning, modeling, and co-teaching, the coaching conversation connected these activities, making discussions more connected to what teachers were experiencing.

Rainwater (chapter 3) examines the perspectives of instructional coaches related to the successes and challenges they experienced while working with teachers. Through the purposeful work of these coaches, they were able to provide one-on-one assistance to teachers—in their classrooms, after teaching, and during other times set aside during the day or after school. The coaches elaborated on not only the barriers they encountered while working with teachers, but also on the successes that they experienced in their work with teachers. We walk away with valuable lessons about how schools can better leverage the work of coaches to support teachers and the instructional program.

Goff (chapter 2) examines the "conversation" as a support structure for beginning teachers. Her findings suggest that first-year teachers found coaches to be helpful when they had positive dispositions and high levels of engagement (See Table 2.2 for the descriptors for positive dispositions and high levels of engagement). Foundation to support is the development of a collegial relationship between the coach and the first-year teacher.

Bolen (chapter 4) examines the specialized learning community and the classroom observations that served as support structures. From these descriptions, we see how these embedded support structures enhanced professional learning.

### Lesson 4: Job-Embedded Coaching Is Coherent

Think back to the program configuration described by Bolen (chapter 4). This program was run by an instructional coach who empowered teachers involved to have tremendous voice in the ways the program operated and how teachers were engaged in learning. The principal entrusted the instructional coach to lead the way with teachers. Coherence is found in the way the program (1) linked monthly meetings to explore notions about teaching that were observed in veteran teacher's classrooms and (2) examined topical areas in the monthly meetings that included areas of concern from the first-year teachers' experiences with children from their classrooms, the curriculum, instruction and its pacing, etc.

Bolen encourages school leaders to step back and look at the professional learning opportunities that the district and school offer. She then offers some questions to ponder. With liberty, some questions have been adapted:

- Is the purpose of professional learning clear and well-articulated?
- Are there opportunities for teams to plan and collaborate?
- Is leadership being built within the teaching corps?
- Do teachers have opportunities to work with others to improve instruction?
- How have teachers been socialized to work with one another?
- What supports are in place to create opportunities for teachers to work with one another?
- Are there any inherent barriers that can prevent teachers from learning with one another?

School leaders can involve others such as assistant principals and teachers in exploring the answers to these questions.

From the answers to these questions can come clarity of not only what is currently in place but also more importantly what is possible. School leaders make professional learning an expectation so that eventually learning from the work is a common practice and not something that happens during, before, and after planning.

Goff's case study (chapter 2) illustrates how coaching conversations can provide coherence. Her research affirms that coaching is a multifaceted job-embedded approach to provide novice teachers with the support they need during their induction years. Although coaches and novices participate in several activities including, co-planning, modeling, and co-teaching, the coaching conversation connects the dots and makes the overall practice cohesive.

Coherence is important because teachers find more value in experiences if they are embedded daily in the work of teaching and learning (Quick, Holtzman, & Chaney, 2009). Job-embedded learning is coherent if it:

1. Is provided within the context of the school—based on the learning needs of students as well as the adults who teach them;

2. Affords teachers with opportunities to learn from the work they are doing;
3. Is situated within programs at the school site—mentoring, induction, coaching, study groups; and
4. Aligns with state, district, and site goals. (Quick et al., 2009)

*Lesson 5: Job-Embedded Coaching Leaves No Coach or Teacher Behind*

Rainwater (chapter 3) examined the barriers and success that instructional coaches experienced as they worked with teachers. Rainwater found that often at the building level, instructional coaches are used as "an extra" administrator, fulfilling duties and responsibilities typically associated with assistant principals. For some of the coaches, this role expansion did not cause concern but for others it did. Goff (chapter 2) was able to distill areas in which coaches need support so that the conditions in which coaching conversations emerge enable coaches to be successful. In both studies, the authors recommended that coaches need ongoing professional development on coaching with a focus on conversations.

With the proliferation of instructional coaches and other support personnel, leaders need to ensure that coaches are provided opportunities for professional learning. Instructional coaches need to learn how to enact their roles in the buildings they serve. Coaches need ongoing professional development around key topical areas including, for example, how to engage in conversations, model various aspects of instruction, and how to conduct classroom observations (peer coaching), and co-teaching. Professional learning needs to continue throughout the year, following the needs of the school and the teachers with which the coaches work.

It is highly doubtful that a school would have more than one instructional coach. Coaches can be encouraged to shadow other coaches in the district, skype as a group to engage in conversations, and attend professional learning opportunities that the state agency, local educational associations, and content specific groups (e.g., mathematics, language arts, science, etc.) held throughout the year.

Instructional coaches typically focus on one or two content areas such as literacy or mathematics; therefore, they need to engage in learning their respective content areas to keep up with new knowledge and other advancements in these areas. Coaches also need professional learning that helps them improve performance skills as in modeling, demonstration lessons, and co-teaching strategies.

From the findings across the three case studies, we can see that coaches need to be encouraged to use their time across three areas: (1) one-on-one work with teachers; (2) work with teams of teachers; and (3) developing, implementing, and monitoring special programs for teachers (e.g., schoolwide peer coaching, book study groups, etc.). In other words, instructional coaches need to be aware of the many forms of job-embedded learning (action research) and the processes (conversations, classroom observations) inherent in them that support teachers in transferring what they are learning into practice.

Now for the elephant in the room. From the findings in Rainwater's study (chapter 3), it is highly suggestive that school leaders need to make a fundamental decision centering on these two questions:

1. Will the instructional coach coach, or will the instructional coach become an add-on administrator?
2. What work is most important for the instructional coach based on your vision for the professional learning for all teachers in the building?

## FINAL THOUGHTS

Coaching is a multifaceted job-embedded approach to providing teachers with the support they need as they face the complexities of teaching. All teachers can benefit from coaching. Given the highly interactive nature of coaching, it has the potential to be a lever for improving instructional practices, one classroom at a time. School leadership has the potential to influence teacher and student learning, and DuFour (2015) reminds us that most especially, "Principals are the critical cog that can support or inhibit both student and adult learning" (p. 223). Leadership does matter.

## SUGGESTED READINGS

Fullan, M., Quinn, J., & Adam, E. (2016). *The taking action guide to building coherence in schools, districts, and systems*. Thousand Oaks, CA: Corwin Press.

Martin. L. E., Kragler, S., Quatrochie, D. J., & Bauerman, K. L. (2014). *Handbook of professional development in education: Successful models and practices, PreK-12*. New York: Guilford Press.

Zepeda, S. J. (2015). *Job-embedded professional development: Support, collaboration, and learning in schools*. New York: Routledge.

Zepeda, S. J. (Ed.). (2018). *Making learning job-embedded: Cases from the field of instructional leadership*. Lanham, MD: Rowman & Littlefield.

# REFERENCES

Allen, J. (2009). *A sense of belonging: Sustaining and retaining new teachers.* Portland, ME: Stenhouse Publishers.

Bandura, A. (1977). *Social learning theory.* New York: General Learning Press.

Baumeister, R. F., & Leary, M. R. (1995). The need to belong: Desire for interpersonal attachment as a fundamental human motivation. *Psychological Bulletin,* 117(3), 497–529. Retrieved from http://www.apa.org/pubs/journals/bul/

Bills, A. M., Giles, D., & Rogers, B. (2016). 'Being in' and 'feeling seen' in professional development as new teachers: The ontological layer(ing) of professional development practice. *Australian Journal of Teacher Education,* 41(2), 106–121. doi: 10.14221/ajte.2016v41n2.7

Bryk, A. S., Sebring, P., Allensworth, E., Luppescu, S., & Easton, J. O. (2010). *Organizing schools for improvement: Lessons from Chicago.* Chicago: University of Chicago Press.

Calvert, L. (2016). *Moving from compliance to agency: What teachers need to make professional learning work.* Oxford, OH: Learning Forward. Retrieved from https://learningforward.org/publications/teacher-agency

Cole, J. (2018). Creating coherence between teacher evaluation and ongoing teacher learning by engaging in collegial goal groups. In S. J. Zepeda (Ed.), *Making learning job-embedded: Cases from the field of instructional leadership* (pp. 35–54). Lanham, MD: Rowman & Littlefield.

Croft, A., Coggshall, J. G., Dolan, M., Powers, E., & Killion, J. (2010). *Job-embedded professional development: What it is, who is responsible, and how to get it done well* [Issue brief]. Washington, DC: National Comprehensive Center for Teacher Quality.

Darling-Hammond, L., Hyler, M. E., & Gardner, M. (2017). *Effective teacher professional development.* Palo Alto, CA: Learning Policy Institute. Retrieved from https://webcache.googleusercontent.com/search?q=cache:hSYNgHwJx_AJ:https://learningpolicyinstitute.org/product/effective-teacher-professional-development-report+&cd=1&hl=en&ct=clnk&gl=us

Darling-Hammond, L., Wei, R., Andree, A., Richardson, N., & Orphanos, S. (2009). *Professional learning in the learning profession: A status report on teacher development in the United States and abroad.* Oxford, OH: National Staff Development Council.

Desimone, L. M. (2009). Improving impact studies of teachers' professional development: Toward better conceptualizations and measures. *Educational Researcher,* 38(3), 181–199. doi: http://doi.org/10.3102/0013189X08331140

Desimone, L. M. (2011). A primer on professional development. *Phi Delta Kappan,* 92(6), 68–71. Retrieved from http://doi.org/10.2307/25822820

Desimone, L. M., & Garet, M. S. (2015). Best practices in teachers' professional development in the United States. *Psychology, Society and Education,* 7(3), 252–263. Retrieved from www.psye.com

Dranitsaris, A. (n.d.). The importance of creating a sense of belonging. [Blog]. *Selfgrowth.com.* Retrieved from http://www.selfgrowth.com/articles/the-importance-of-creating-a-sense-of-belonging-in-organizations

DuFour, R. (2015). *In praise of American educators: And how they can become even better.* Bloomington, IN: Solution Tree Press.

Glazerman, S., Isenberg, E., Dolfin, S., Bleeker, M., Johnson, A., Grider, M., et al. (2010). *Impacts of comprehensive teacher induction: Final results from a randomized controlled study.* Washington, DC: National Center for Education, Evaluation, and Regional Assistance, Institute of Education Sciences, U.S. Department of Education.

Goddard, Y. L., & Goddard, R. D. (2007). A theoretical and empirical investigation of teacher collaboration for school improvement and student achievement in public elementary schools. *Teacher College Record*, 109(4), 877–896. Retrieved from http://www.tcrecord.org/

Guskey, T. R. (2014). Planning professional learning. *Educational Leadership*, 71(8), 10–16. Retrieved from http://www.ascd.org/publications/educational-leadership.aspx

Huppert, M. (2017). Employees share what gives them a sense of belonging at work. [Blog]. *Linkedin Talent Blog.* Retrieved from https://business.linkedin.com/talent-solutions/blog/company-culture/2017/employees-share-what-gives-them-a-sense-of-belonging-at-work

Johnson, S., & Kardos, S. M. (2002). Keeping new teachers in mind. *Educational Leadership*, 59(6), 12–16. Retrieved from http://www.ascd.org/publications/educational-leadership.aspx

Kardos, S. M., & Johnson, S. M. (2007). On their own and presumed expert: New teachers' experiences with their colleagues. *Teachers College Record*, 109(9), 2083–2106. Retrieved from www.tcrecord.org

Kardos, S. M., Johnson, S. M., Peske, H. G., Kauffman, D., & Liu, E. (2001). Counting on colleagues: New teachers encounter the professional cultures of their schools. *Educational Administration Quarterly*, 37(2), 250–290. doi: https://doi.org/10.1177/00131610121969316

Kelly, K. M. (2001). Individual differences in reactions to rejection. In M. R. Leary (Ed.), *Interpersonal rejection* (pp. 291–315). New York: Oxford University Press.

Knowles, M. (1973). *The adult learner: A neglected species.* Houston: Gulf Professional Publishing.

Knowles, M. S., Holton, E. F., & Swanson, R. A. (2011). *The adult learner.* Burlington, MA: Elsevier.

Learning Theories. (n.d.). *Social learning theory* (Bandura). Retrieved from https://www.learning-theories.com/social-learning-theory-bandura.html

Lortie, D. (1975). *Schoolteacher: A sociological study.* Chicago: University of Chicago Press.

Louis, K. S., Marks, H. M., & Kruse, S. (1996). Teachers' professional community in restructuring schools. *American Educational Research Journal*, 33(4), 757–798. doi: https://doi.org/10.3102/00028312033004757

Maslow, A. H. (1943). A theory of human motivation. *Psychological Review*, 50(4), 370–396. doi: http://dx.doi.org/10.1037/h0054346

Newmann, F., & Wehlage, G. (1995). *Successful school restructuring: A report to the public and educators*. Madison, WI: Center on Organization and Restructuring of Schools.

Qian, H., Youngs, P., & Frank, K. (2013). Collective responsibility for learning: Effects on interactions between novice teachers and colleagues. *Journal of Educational Change*, 14(4), 445–464. doi: 10.1007/s10833-013-9210-0

Quick, H., Holtzman, D., & Chaney, K. (2009). Professional development and instructional practice: Conceptions and evidence of effectiveness. *Journal of Education for Students Placed at Risk (JESPAR)*, 14(1), 45–71.

Rogers, C. R. (1951). *Client-centered therapy: Its current practice, implications, and theory.* Boston: Houghton Mifflin.

SimplyPsychology (n.d.) Maslow's hierarchy of needs. Retrieved from http://www.simplypsychology.org/maslow.html

Vicarious Reinforcement and Imitative Learning. (n.d.). Social learning theory: Understanding Bandura's theory of learning. Retrieved from https://d2l.deakin.edu.au/d2l/eP/presentations/presentation_preview_popup.d2l?presId=96946

Vygotsky, L. (1978). *Mind and society.* Cambridge, MA: Harvard University Press.

Zepeda, S., & Ponticell, J. A. (1997). First-year teachers at risk: A study of induction at three high schools. *The High School Journal*, *81*(1), 8-21. Retrieved from http://soe.unc.edu/hsj/issues.php

Zepeda, S. J. (2015). *Job-embedded professional development: Support, collaboration, and learning in schools*. New York: Routledge.

Zepeda, S. J. (2017). Course syllabus for learning communities and staff development. Athens, GA: University of Georgia.

# Index

97

# About the Editor

**Sally J. Zepeda**, Ph.D., is professor at the University of Georgia in the Department of Lifelong Education, Administration, and Policy. She teaches courses related to instructional supervision and theory, teacher evaluation, and professional learning. She is a former high school English and speech teacher, middle and high school assistant principal, principal, and director of special programs. She has published thirty books and countless articles and book chapters.

Zepeda's most recent books include *Instructional Supervision: Applying Tools and Concepts* (4th edition) that was simultaneously translated into Turkish. Other books include *Job-Embedded Professional Development: Support, Collaboration, and Learning in Schools*, coedited (with Jeffrey Glanz), *Supervision: New Perspectives for Theory and Practice*; and *Making Learning Job-Embedded: Cases from the Field of Instructional Leadership*. She is presently coediting the *Handbook of Educational Supervision*.

Zepeda has worked with many school systems in the United States and overseas, especially the Middle East, to support teacher and leader development. She has received numerous local and national awards including the University Council of Educational Administration (UCEA) Master Professor Award.

# Chapter Author Biographies

**Susan Hare Bolen**, Ph.D., is an elementary school teacher in the Clarke County School District in Athens, Georgia. Bolen has taught children in Alabama, California, Kentucky, North Carolina, and Georgia. She has worked as a classroom teacher in grades one through five, an elementary instructional coach, a reading support teacher, and a summer school administrator. Bolen has been a practitioner for twenty-six years and currently serves her school and community by sitting on her school's Instructional Leadership Team and the Local School Governance Team.

**Lakesha Robinson Goff**, Ed.D., served as an assistant principal in the Atlanta Public Schools for the past two years before relocating to the Dallas–Fort Worth area. Her research interests include novice teacher development and coaching. Goff served as a middle school mathematics teacher and induction coach for more than a decade. She also worked as a Manager of Teacher Leadership Development with Teach for America. Goff has extensive experience developing induction models, coaching educators, and delivering professional development including serving as a guest facilitator at the Oprah Winfrey Leadership Academy for Girls in South Africa. Goff is a recipient of the Ray E. Bruce Academic Support Award from the Department of Lifelong Education, Administration, and Policy at the University of Georgia.

**Angela K. Rainwater**, Ed.D., is assistant professor in the Education Department at Toccoa Falls College in Toccoa Falls, Georgia. She was previously an instructional coach and classroom teacher in public school systems before moving into higher education. Rainwater received the Ray E. Bruce Academic Support Award from the Department of Lifelong Education, Administration, and Policy at the University of Georgia.